Four and One

Theresa Ann Boddie

Kingdom Builders Publications LLC

Copyright © 2020 Theresa Ann Boddie

Kingdom Builders Publications

All rights reserved. No part of this book may be reproduced or transmitted in any form or by any means without written permission from the author.

ISBN: 978-0-578-70849-2 Soft Copy

Library of Congress Control Number: 2020910617

Printed in the USA

Authored by

Theresa Ann Boddie

Editor

Dr. Lakisha S. Forrester

Kingdom Builders Publications

Cover Design

LoMar Designs

Picture for cover

ID 52853376 © Natareal | Dreamstime.com

Other pictures

From the personal library of Theresa Ann Boddie

PREFACE

FOUR and ONE is a story about a young black couple growing up in the South. They met as children, lived in the same neighborhood, and went to the same school. They had a son right out of high school. They later married, but money was tight, so they both went back to school to major in their career jobs. An unexpected pregnancy caught them by surprise and they got more than they expected.

CONTENTS

	Preface	iii
	Acknowledgments	vi
	Dedication	vii
	Disclaimer	viii
1	Growing Up In a Low-Income Household	9
2	Serving the Lord with Gladness	12
3	With This Ring	17
4	Starting a New Life Together	55
5	More Than a Bundle	73
6	College Criminals	106
7	Going Through, When It's All Said and Done	243
	Epilogue	259
	Final Point	262
	Notes	263
	About the Author	264

ACKNOWLEDGMENTS

I acknowledge you, my Heavenly Father, for all of the many blessings that you have bestowed upon me, and for giving me vision, health, strength, and lots of love.

When I look around and think back on what could have been, whether it was good or bad, all I can say is, "Thank You, Lord!"

I am thankful for my son Von. He has given me the push that I needed many times. "Mommy, you need to get those books out there. You never know how far God is going to bless you," is what he would say to me. Thanks, Von! I love you, fella.

Finally, to anyone who's been bullied, take it to the Cross. Call out their names to our Father, stand firm, and say, "God, you said you would make my enemies flee seven ways. You said you would make them my footstool, and you also said they would be cut down like grass."

God will do what no other can do. He can heal your wounds and halt the enemy's plan against your life. Just try Him for yourself, be patient, and wait to see how the Master works.

DEDICATION

To my brother, Reginald Anthony Boddie (3/8/1956 - 8/19/2017), as hard as it is to type this, I just want to say that the love we shared as sister and brother will forever live in my heart. You protected me, even if it caused you to fight others for me. May you rest knowing that you are now healed and sitting around the throne of the King of all kings. I love you, Reggie.

DISCLAIMER

This work is fictitious and created from the author's mind. It was written for you, the reader, for your enjoyment and entertainment. Any similarity with the events or characters (either alive or deceased) to real life (unless otherwise noted) is merely coincidental.

GROWING UP IN A LOW-INCOME HOUSEHOLD

Chapter One

Back in the late sixties, a lot of families in the South struggled. They did what they had to do to make ends meet and to care for their families.

The houses were detached. Back then, some didn't have toilets inside the house until the later years.

The neighbors all knew one another and it was not uncommon to borrow anything from your neighborly friend, like a cup of milk, sugar, butter, clothes, or whatever.

Living in the South, they have what is known as southern hospitality, which means showing nothing but love.

Some families had to walk a great distance to work unless someone nearby had a car. They all would pile into that car and get dropped off at their work location or somewhere nearby.

Schoolwork was a big focus in most of the households because some of the older parents had to cut their education short. They either had to work or stay at home to tend to the children.

Some of the stay-at-home moms did odd jobs around the neighborhood, like doing other people's laundry and ironing their clothes. Some would cook and clean another person's house. This would all take place while the children were in school, and if the mom had a small child, she would take the child along with her to work.

The Jackson family and the Waller family were very close friends. Both families had six children. Aaron, the oldest child in the Jackson's household, dated Anita, the Waller's oldest daughter, while they were both in the 12th grade. When you saw one, you would see the other. They were both ushers in the church and they sang in the choir.

Aaron and Anita had similar dreams of growing up and becoming someone big and making lots of money. Aaron never liked the struggle his parents went through. He always said that when he got older he was going to care for his family and give them more than they were able to give to him. They both dreamed that they would become financially independent so they could help their families become stress-free.

Most times, the clothes and shoes they wore were not new, but they were passed down from someone else. They were always clean and when they stepped out of the house, they were looking good.

The neighborhood was peaceful where the Wallers and the Jacksons lived. There were no crimes. They all got along with one another. They cared for each other. No one had room to look down or criticize anyone because most of them were in the same boat. They all struggled and worked hard to get what they had.

If anyone in the neighborhood needed work done, whether it was inside or outside of the house, they didn't have to look far. Most of the men learned a trade of their own by watching others. There were carpenters, drywallers, painters, gardeners, mechanics, and plumbers. There was always one person who was multitalented and knew how to do it all. Although those skills paid very good money, many still struggled.

The town they lived in was small and the people did not have much to do on the weekends. There was one movie theater, one club, and a bowling alley. One family had a swimming pool, so that was the house where most of the children would hang out.

The girls learned how to sew, cook, clean, knit, and do hair, while the boys learned how to work and be responsible and respectable.

In the South, lots of people grew most of their food, like the vegetables they ate, different kinds of leafy greens, peas, carrots, cucumbers, onions, peppers, string beans, squash, tomatoes, and potatoes. They raised the meat they ate, like chickens, cows, and pigs. The pigs grew to be big hogs. Back then, you could eat the pigs from the rooter to the tooter, and that was from the head to the tail; they ate it all. There was a lot of meat that could be eaten from a hog, such as sausage, ham, bacon, pork chops, and ribs to name a few. Most of the fruits they ate were grown, and what they did not grow, they would go to the market to buy.

During the summer, air conditioning was not one of the luxury items in their houses, but they did have fans back then. The heat did not stop their mission to keep pressing on. They would just drink lots of ice-cold water, tea, or lemonade. Some days it would get scorching hot, but the pollution and the poor air quality were not as bad back then. At night, it was hard to sleep, so they would fan themselves with a piece of paper until they fell asleep.

Serving the Lord with Gladness

Chapter Two

Some of the children in the lower income families missed out on a lot because the income was not there. But they knew that God would bring them through it all, and with their faith, He did! Every Sunday morning, they got up, ate breakfast, and went to church, serving the Lord with gladness.

When you grow up in a small country town with little to do, most of your time was spent in church. The church that almost everyone in the area attended was an old wooden church named Mount Anna Missionary Baptist Church. There, all were welcomed to give their testimony and praise unto God. This building sat on more than ten acres of land. As the congregation sang and the deacons prayed, many would tap on the floor or the rails or pat their feet. The least bit of noise that was made sounded like they had instruments like bongos and congas. Their singing sounded like archangels. When they prayed, they would go up until the power of the Lord came down. They all looked forward to Sunday because they knew that they would feast and fill up off the Word all week long.

A lot of the members were at church more than once a week. They had Bible study, prayer service, choir practice, meetings for the different committees, funerals, weddings, and what have you.

Most of the members were active in the church. The families knew that when all else failed, they could look to the hills for all the help they needed; they knew that the Savior was not far away.

Mount Anna wanted a baptism pool and air conditioning. Of course, that would be a big project that would cost a lot of money. Many times, the board members came together to meet and put their heads together to come up with ways to raise money. Raising money for the building fund took lots of time, patience, and creativity, but that never stopped them. It seemed like they never got tired.

Most of the members and congregation struggled financially, but that did not stop them from giving and paying their tithes. Most of the monies collected went towards the building fund when they had fundraisers.

They would have lots of church functions like bake sales and selling dinners. They would even have a flea market where anyone could rent a table and sell goods that they no longer wanted. The church would get a fee for the table and the rest of the money would go to the person who was using that table. They loved a good bargain, so they looked forward to that time of the year.

When the church would have a carnival with rides, they would have a chicken contest. That's when the chickens' owners would dress the chickens up. The person with the best dressed chicken would win a prize. They also had hog rides. They would put a saddle on the hog's back and the children's parents would pay to let their children ride the hog.

The church would have fashion and talent shows. They would have youth day and youth night, which would allow the children to come together and have fun all night long. People from near and far would participate in lots of the activities that Mount Anna had. Mount Anna was that one church that had so much going on. You could get saved with God's Word and have a good time, all the time.

When Mount Anna would have "Friends and Family Day," old members that used to come to church at one time and they stopped for whatever reason — some moved, some worked on Sundays — would be drawn back. The members would invite people from out of town. They would have dinner after service and sometimes a guest artist would sing. What a mighty good time they would have at this all-day event.

Mount Anna would also sponsor bus trips, and they would visit different states to sightsee for the day. A lot of times the pastor or the choir would be invited to another church; this was when Mount Anna would show up and show out in big numbers. Sometimes the whole congregation would go along with the pastor. Service was always good at home and away. That's why most of the members looked forward to Sunday morning.

Back in those days, you really were baptized in the lake or river so that you could have your name in the Lamb's book or records. Being saved was and still is a good thing.

Back then, daddies and granddaddies would pastor at the same church. When they prayed, they would send up some timber. The sweat would run down their faces, their mouths would become dry, but they did not stop until they said, "Amen," and every concern was sent up to the Lord.

The people in this town would come to church on Sunday. In attendance would be the pastor, a few deacons, the clerk, ushers, the men's choir, the senior choir, the youth and young adult choirs, the finance person, the hospitality committee, the secretary, the treasurer, the trustees, and the members.

When the church would have wonderful biblical plays, they would dress like the people in the Bible.

The church believed in some of the holidays. They would practice and prepare to have a program ahead of time, no matter what holiday it was. They started making the clothing early. Whether it was narrating the program or whatever they did for that holiday, they had fun doing it. They all got a biblical lesson and they kept it holy.

After a couple of years, Mount Anna had grown with new members, and the new addition was on the way. The church held a meeting with all the officers and members. When the meeting was called to order, they opened up with a prayer. They went on to say that the groundbreaking ceremony would be two weeks from that day. As they passed out the agenda, with everything in detail, they discussed the finances. They discussed building the new church and how long it would take. They talked about the whole process and everything it would take to get the job done. They planned to use all of the laborers in the town and they asked for volunteers. Aaron and Dwayne were the first two who raised their hands, along with some of the others.

Graduation day for the seniors in the town was an exciting day for the 12th graders and their families. Even though Aaron and Anita had big dreams for the future, they planned to put their college education on hold to work and save money to help the family; but that did not stop them from dreaming and planning.

The day the building of the new church started; all were excited. Progress moved swiftly because they worked from sunup until sundown. They prayed each day before they started work and they prayed after they finished for the day.

With the construction of the new building being an ongoing project, they decided to keep the old church standing so they could later remodel it. Sunday service and everything else were still being held in the old church like normal.

Building the new church was done meticulously with care. They dug the hole, laid the pipes for the plumbing, and poured the concrete. While the workers allowed the concrete to harden, they started framing the building. The new sanctuary was going to be large. There was going to be a gym inside for the children, a kitchen and fellowship hall, meeting rooms, and a room for the nurses of the church. On the outside, there would be plenty of parking and a picnic area with a playground.

With the money that was raised, they were able to buy two busses for the church; so they no longer had to charter busses when they had engagements away from church.

On Sunday morning, while in service, the clerk, Mrs. Ruby Robinson, gave the announcements. During that time, she would always say, "Our new church is getting close to being complete." They would all clap their hands after she made that statement. One Sunday, she asked if there was anyone who would like to help out with the decorations for the fellowship hall. They needed pictures or paintings, curtains or drapes, and anything else that would beautify the new church. She asked those who were interested to sign their name after service and let them know what they planned on doing to help.

When the construction finally ended on the new Mount Anna Missionary Baptist Church, they held service in a mighty way.

WITH THIS RING

Chapter Three

Aaron and Anita, the newly graduates, were so much in love, until it hurt them to be apart from each other. They would sneak out of the house while everyone was sleeping and go off to be alone.

They started having sex and the next month Anita's cycle did not come. They both panicked and did not know what to do, so Anita called her auntie who lived in Washington, D.C., to tell her what was going on.

Most people back in the South only wanted the best for their children. Getting pregnant just finishing high school or while still in school was a no-no. If that happened, many parents would send the girls away to live with a relative and made up a reason why they were not around.

Some families would give the baby to a relative and the baby would become theirs. He or she would grow up and not know that his or her aunt, uncle, or cousin, was their actual birth parent. It was a hush-hush secret, something that was kept silent to everyone.

When Anita talked with her auntie, both she and Aaron already knew what would take place so they wanted to get a jump ahead of their parents.

The couple sat and discussed many things; they expressed their feelings about the future. They talked, yelled, laughed, and cried together.

Aaron assured Anita that even though she was carrying their child, he would be with her all of the way.

They talked about their dreams that were now put on hold. Anita vocalized her concerns, "What about our college education? What about the dream of me becoming a nurse and you becoming a lawyer? What about owning our own home? What about having money to help our family? What about us having all of the nice things we always talked about? Who's going to help us raise a child when we depend on our parents to care for us? What about that, Aaron?"

"Gee, you sure threw a lot out to me all at one time. Where is your faith, Nita?" He said it with a big laugh, but Anita did not find any humor in it.

"I'm in no laughing mood right now. I am serious," she said.

Then Aaron said, "So am I. Like I said, where is your faith? Don't you know God has big plans in our lives? As long as we continue to praise Him, thank Him, and let Jesus guide us, there's nothing He won't do for us, Nita. Nothing is too hard for God.

"Anita, let me answer each question as you gave them to me. First, you said, 'What about our college education?' We are both going to go to college. Maybe not this year, but we will get our degrees in the fields we talked about. With what's going on now, the baby, look, don't worry about that. You or both of us may end up going to school in another state, but we will become college students.

"After that you said, let me see. Picture this, Aaron Jackson, Attorney-at-Law, will soon come, and calling Nurse Anita Jackson. And yes, I said Anita Jackson. We will be husband and wife. You know how our parents are. I will marry you right now if I have to. So, this is what you want, right? To be a nurse and my wife. And what I want to be is your husband and an attorney. Oh trust and believe, it will happen.

"As for our dream home, we will work and save to have the house of our dreams. Every penny that we can save, we will.

"Now, I think you said, 'What about helping our family?' And the answer to that is, as long as we can help, we will. Our parents have always given us what we needed, even if it was a struggle for them to get it. They deserve to get all that we can give to them, with love.

"As far as the things we always wanted and talked about will come. When we move into our dream home, the only things that will be used are some of our clothes, believe that. We have family who would love to care for our child, and if our parents have to do it, they will be paid something for babysitting. Now, I think I answered every question you asked in order. How do you like that, Mrs. Jackson?"

When Aaron said, "Mrs. Jackson" to Anita, he tapped her on the leg and winked his eye. She smiled and said, "I love you, Aaron," and then Aaron said, "I love you more."

Anita's auntie that she called was Patsy. She and her husband Chris were both doctors. They had two children, a boy and a girl, and their names were Dallas and Spencer.

Patsy told Anita not to tell her parents about the baby right now. She told her that she had two bedrooms, a den, and that the apartment in her basement was empty. She told her that she and the baby were welcomed to stay as long as they like.

Three months went by and Anita's mom, Henrietta, who buys all of their personal items, noticed that Anita's sanitary pads had not been touched. Her first reaction was to go into panic mode, but then she took a deep breath and said to herself, "Ok Henri, we're not going to panic and make a scene. You have other children in the house. Let me call Pat." So Henrietta walked over to the phone and called her sister Patsy. Patsy could always defuse any situation and turn it around for the positive.

Patsy's home phone rang, but no one answered. So Henrietta hung up the phone and dialed it again. After the phone rang a few times, Patsy answered it, "Good morning."

"Where were you? I called two times," Henrietta said.

"Calm down, I just got out of the shower. How are you?" Patsy said.

"I'm not sure. You know–" Henrietta paused. "You know, I think Anita is–"

Patsy cut her off by saying, "Pregnant," with a high-pitched voice.

Henrietta said, "Yes, she is. How do you know?"

Still with the high pitch in her voice, Patsy said, "She called me a few months ago."

"A few months ago, what? A few months ago, I am shocked," Henri said.

"Well, don't be, Henri. First, you're going to stop repeating everything I say. Now, I know Nita is your child and my niece, but when she thought that she was expecting, she called me and we have been talking all the time. You and Al sometimes take things and turn it into a big mess. You all know how you do," Patsy said.

Then Henri said, "I had no idea until I noticed that Lisa and Melanie are using their pads, but little Miss Anita Waller's bag of napkins has not been touched."

"There you go with that little Miss Anita junk. Females get pregnant all the time. It happened before she and Aaron were ready. Don't look down on them. Keep showing your love towards them in every way. I mean it, you know I look at situations differently. Maybe that's why she came to me. Not saying that you would have did things wrong, but I'm glad she called me early. Anita has seen Dr. Porter; this should be her third visit with him coming up soon," Pat said.

"I was going to mention that, sis. I thank you, Al and I both thank you. But, am I very happy? No. Am I ready to be a grandma? No," said

Henri.

"Well, you better start getting ready," Patsy said.

"What's going to happen now? You know how people talk," Henrietta said.

Patsy said, "Yes, I know how they talk and I don't worry about them. Most of those talkers can barely handle their own family problems.

"What Chris and I plan to do is come visit for a few days. Then we are going to drive to Disney World. If it's ok, the children want their cousins to come along with them. I'm going to call Leslie and Lamont to see if their kids want to come along. We are going to drive the mobile home but stay in the family home for two weeks, so we will have enough room. When we return, I guess we will bring Nita back home with us. Now, that's our plan, we will see how things go."

"What month are we talking about?" Henrietta asked.

"Well, it won't be right now. I think that's a little too soon for Nita to leave home. Let's wait until next month," Patsy said.

"So what is she going to be doing while she's at your home?" Henrietta asked.

"Well, she's either going to enroll in school or work. I think going to school would be best. That way she can start studying towards her degree. And after the baby comes, she can care for the baby and still study," Patsy answered.

Patsy then said, "Hey look, I am off today and I have a lot to do so we will talk later, but remember, we all made mistakes. You stay cool. Love you, sis. Bye."

After Sunday service, Anita's mom gave her a hug and said, "I'm not mad at you, but I am a little disappointed. I didn't want you to do like I did and tie yourself down with children. I wanted you to start college while you are young, get your degree, and live the life of your dreams."

Anita said, "Mama, I will follow my dreams. I'm still young and this is just a setback. It's only for a minute. I won't let myself down, so I won't let you down. I love you, Mama."

"I love you too, baby girl," Henrietta said.

During dinner, Aaron stopped by Anita's house and asked to speak with her parents.

"Mr. and Mrs. Waller, you both know I love Anita with all my heart. While we are all here, I'm asking for your daughter's hand in marriage, and I'm asking for both of your blessings," Aaron said.

Mr. Waller stood up and said to Aaron, "Come here, young man." He grabbed Aaron, gave him a hug, and said, "I don't have to welcome you into the family because you have always been family. But one thing I want to say is, love my child, just like I love her. Listen to her when she calls. Keep your communication open always. Let Nita know you love her daily. Always keep Christ in your lives." Then he looked at Anita and Aaron and said, "Make sure you both raise my grandchild right. Oh yes, we know."

Both Aaron and Anita were stunned. All they could say was, "Yes sir."

"Now when is the wedding?" Anita's dad asked.

Aaron said, "Well, I have to talk with my family, and we all can get the plans on the way."

Anita jumped up and said, "Yes, I am so happy," with a big smile.

When Aaron got home, he talked with his parents and told them that he asked Anita's parents for her hand in marriage.

Lamont, Aaron's dad, said, "We knew you would do the right thing, son, with having a baby on the way. We're proud of you because you are owning up to your responsibility and I know you will make a good husband and father."

Aaron looked at his parents and said, "How did y'all know about the baby?"

Leslie, Aaron's mom, said, "Son, we are your parents. We know our children and we see what goes on in this house and around the corner. Now when is the wedding?"

Aaron answered, "As soon as possible."

"Well then, I will talk with Henri so that we can start doing our part," his mom said.

Aaron and Anita went to the church before Bible study started to talk with the pastor, Reverend Dr. Anthony Penny.

As they walked into the church, Pastor Penny said, "Well hello, Brother Aaron and Sister Anita. You're early. Prayer service doesn't start for another hour and a half!"

"I know, Pastor Penny," Aaron said. "Anita and I wanted to talk with you before the service starts."

"Well, come into my office," Pastor Penny said.

As they walked inside the office, he said, "Have a seat. How can I help both of you?"

"Pastor Penny, Anita and I want to get married –"

Pastor cut him off and said, "Excuse me, son. Let us pray first. Shall we bow our heads? With all hearts clear, Heavenly Father, this is your manservant, coming to you on behalf of two of your children. God you know both of them. You've known them even before they were conceived. I pray that every word that comes from my mouth would be what you would have me to say. Lead them and guide them. Keep them on the straight and narrow path. Let them always know that you are an awesome God, and besides you there is no other. Continue to let their light so shine as they have since I've known them. Keep them planted and well-grounded. Let them always acknowledge you as their Lord and Savior, and you will grant them the desires of their hearts, in Jesus' name I pray, Amen.

And they all said, "Amen."

"Well, son, marriage is a big step. Are you sure this is what you both want?" Pastor Penny asked.

They both answered, "Yes sir."

"Now I know you two care for each other, it shows. Are you sure you don't want to get your college degrees first?" Pastor Penny said.

"Well, Pastor Penny, Anita and I are expecting a baby and we know how everyone will look down on us. So before she moves to D.C. and before the baby comes, I want the mother and our child to have my last name. Pastor, I plan to spend the rest of my life with this young lady sitting right here," Aaron said.

"Well, son, since you put it that way, yes, I will marry you. Sister Anita, you have my blessings. You are a beautiful couple. Now how soon are we talking?" Pastor Penny asked.

"We are making plans now with our parents. We will stay in touch with you," Aaron said.

"Make sure that you do. If I can help in any way, just let me know," Pastor Penny said.

Anita and Aaron both said, "We will, Pastor, thanks."

As they walked out of the pastor's study, still having time before Bible study, they left the church and walked home. Anita felt the baby kick for the first time. She stopped, with her mouth wide open and her eyes stretched wide, and said, "Aaron feel it. The baby just kicked."

Aaron put his hands on Anita's stomach. He felt the kick and said, "Hi little one, it's Daddy, we are so happy to know that you are growing, and soon you will be in Mommy's and Daddy's arms. You are going to know nothing but love."

As they were walking home, they talked about school. Anita said, "You know having a baby doesn't have to be all bad. I know I am not the only person that went to college pregnant. Why don't we look into it? That way we can both start school, find a job, and start a new life together. If I go to D.C., then you won't be around the baby much."

Then Aaron said, "I thought about that and I was going to talk with you once I gathered all of my thoughts. What I was thinking is enrolling at one of the colleges in the D.C. area, like Virginia or maybe Maryland.

"I'm going to call Aunt Patsy and Uncle Chris to see if it's ok if I come to live in their home with my family and see if they know any lawyers in the area. Maybe I can get a job working for them. You never know, God answers prayers."

Anita smiled and said, "Yes, He does."

Aaron and Anita went to Aaron's home first. When they walked into the door, Aaron's mom said, "I am so excited. I have been talking with Patsy and Henri all day. Now Nita, you have to unglue yourself from Aaron for just a little while so that we can make all the arrangements. We have a lot of planning to do in a short time."

Anita said, "I know, Mrs. Jackson, I am ready to work with you and my mom in all of the planning."

"Ok, so tomorrow, we are going to start early. Your mom, you, and I are going to get some things taken care of. I am going to give y'all a call bright and early in the morning. So get some sleep and be ready. Now go on, Bible study starts soon. But I'm glad you stopped by. I'll see you at the church house," said Mrs. Jackson.

"Yes ma'am, I will," Anita said.

Aaron and Anita left his home and they went back to church for Bible study. Every week at Bible study, they learned about God's Word from a chapter taken from the Bible. Pastor Penny started with Genesis and ended with Revelation. First, they discussed the past week's lesson that was given to them in homework form.

Everyone was excited about learning the Bible. So many people came out for Bible study. It was so overwhelming, in a good way, to see all of the saints come together on a weekday.

The next morning, Leslie, Aaron's mom, got up bright and early. She showered and started to cook breakfast. While preparing what she was going to cook, she called Henrietta. Henrietta answered the phone and she sounded like she was still sleeping.

Leslie yelled in the phone, "Break time is over, time to rise and shine! Get up!"

Henri said, "I'm up. You are one of the loudest women I know. Was that for me to hear or the whole neighborhood?"

Leslie said, "It's for whoever is going to help us get this wedding planning started, so come on now, I'm cooking breakfast. Y'all are welcome to eat over here."

Henri's response was, "Let me jump in the shower. I'll see you in a few. I'm bringing the kids, so make enough."

Then Leslie said, "I don't care. You can bring your husband too; he needs to know what's going on."

Henri's response was, "I will, goodbye."

Leslie yelled to her husband and children, "Get up, I'm fixing breakfast! Nita and her family are eating with us this morning, so go into the bathroom, shower or wash up, and get dressed; we have a lot to do."

While Leslie continued to prepare breakfast for her family and Anita's family, about 45 minutes later, she got a knock at the door. A voice said, "Knock, knock, coming in. Good morning." That was Henri's voice coming in the house.

Leslie said, "Well, it's about time. Come on back. You can help me put the food on the children's plates and they can go sit outside and eat."

While the Jacksons and the Wallers all sat at the table eating breakfast, they discussed the wedding. They talked about the colors of the clothing that would be worn and whether the wedding was going to be big or small. They discussed the food and the day that would be set.

The colors Aaron and Anita decided on were silver and gold. Everyone in the town knew each other and they did not want to leave anyone out, so they agreed to announce their wedding at Sunday service during the announcements. Whoever wanted to attend were welcomed, so they did not make a list for the invites. They all agreed to have the reception outside on the lawn of the church where there were two fire pits for grilling and plenty of tables with benches. There was even one section that was covered just in case it rained.

Trying to save money, Anita's youngest sister, Andreya was going to be the flower girl, and Aaron's youngest brother, Michael was to be the ring bearer. They wanted a best man and a maid of honor, so they decided on Dwayne, Aaron's best friend, and Corky, Anita's best friend. They decided to have Aaron's dad to escort his wife and Anita's mom down the aisle together. Anita's dad was going to walk her down the aisle.

So Lamont, Aaron's dad, said, "I guess old Chuck-Chuck is headed to the slaughterhouse. Now that we've gotten the pork out of the way, what other meat are we having?"

Alfred, Anita's dad, said, "Big as Chuck-Chuck is, we don't need any more meat; he will feed everybody in this town and the next town."

They all got a laugh out of that.

But then Monty (short for Lamont) said to Anita's dad (who they called "Ail"), "You know, Ail, you might be right. What other meat should we have since this reception is going to be a cook-out? Why not chicken, hot dogs, and hamburgers?"

They all agreed on having the chicken, hot dogs, and hamburgers, along with Chuck-Chuck. Then they talked about the starch, vegetables, and the cake.

Henri said, "I'll have Pearlie, she's Anita's great aunt, to make the cake and the cornbread. She's the one that everybody goes to when they want all different kinds of desserts made. She also works at the town's bakery."

Greens, string beans, and coleslaw would be the veggies. They were also going to have potato salad, macaroni and cheese, along with baked beans.

"Now we all like to drink some good old cold iced tea or lemonade. Everybody loves iced tea. Do we all agree?" Leslie said.

They all said, "We agree."

"Now that we have the food and drinks squared away, what about the clothes? I'm not buying a silver or gold suit. Are you, Ail?" Lamont said.

Ail said, "No, I am not. The best I can do is my black usher, deacon, and choir suit. That is what I'm going to wear. I can get a silver or gold shirt and tie. Do you agree, Monty? We both can go in together for this silver and gold. You buy one color and I'll buy the other. Now how does that sound?"

Lamont said, "Sounds good to me; that's what we'll do."

Then Aaron said, "That's all good. Ok, all the men wear white shirts and black suits. One dad will wear the gold tie, while the other one, a silver tie. Mike, Dwayne, and I, same fabric for the tie, handkerchief, and cummerbund!"

"Oh, we can make those, Les," Henri said. "Now what are the mothers going to wear?"

Then Anita said, "What we would like as far as the clothing is, Aaron's bow tie and cummerbund will be silver and gold. We just talked about the dads' clothing. The mothers, I would like you to wear one or the other color. The flower girl will have a white dress with silver and gold flowers on it; the ring bearer, a silver and gold bow tie; the best man wears a tie. Both Mike and Dwayne will wear a handkerchief in the pocket. As for me, I'll discuss it later, along with the maid of honor."

Monty looked at Henri and Leslie and said, "From what I see, it doesn't look like the men need to spend much money. Do (he pointed his finger looking at each lady) you or you have a silver or gold dress?"

Then Leslie said, "Tell him, Henri."

"Because we are the mothers, we want to look beautiful. We might have silver and gold in our closet but we may not want to wear it. We know how to sew and we can make what we plan to wear. We're going to the fabric store anyway because Nita's gown will have to be made," Henrietta said.

Then Leslie said, "Now that every belly is full, the ladies need to go into town so that we can look at the fabric and get started. But first, everyone is going to help clean up my kitchen before we go anywhere."

Aaron got up and said, "Come on men, let's get the kitchen cleaned."

They got up and grabbed the plates and glasses off the table. They walked into the kitchen and the children brought their dishes into the house.

Meanwhile, the ladies went into the living room and sat down, discussing quietly what they planned to wear.

Anita said, "I want a white gown. (Nita's mom and Mrs. Jackson looked at her with crazy eyes.) Yes, white. I haven't had the baby yet, so I can wear white with silver and gold trim. It will be beautiful; and Corky has a beautiful gown that has all the colors of the wedding in it."

Then Anita put her hands over her mouth and said, "We forgot the flowers. What about the flowers? Do you think Mrs. Helen will do the flowers for me?"

Aaron's mom said, "Calm down, child; that's what she does. We haven't heard talk around town about any funerals or weddings, so she can't be that busy. When we go into town, we will run by Helen's house and talk with her."

After the men had washed the dishes, dried them, and put them away, they went into the living room and said, "Now what y'all have planned?"

Anita's mom said, "We were just talking about the flowers, and that was something we did not talk about at the table."

Aaron's dad said, "We did not have to talk about flowers, you know?"

"We know that," Aaron's mom said. "Mrs. Helen will do the flowers. That's how she makes her money. You think she's going to turn down the job? I'm just saying that we are going to run by her house before we go into town."

Aaron's dad said, "Well if y'all had it under control, why didn't Henri say that? I could have saved my words."

"Ladies, shall we get started?" Leslie said.

So the ladies left the house and got into the car. Anita's mom drove up two blocks, made a right turn, and drove past two houses. Then she started blowing the horn and yelling out the window.

"Hey, Mrs. Helen, how are you?" Leslie said.

Mrs. Helen yelled back and said, "I'm fine. Y'all get out of that car and come sit with me for a spell."

So they parked and got out of the car and started walking towards Mrs. Helen's yard. They opened the gate and walked into the yard.

Mrs. Helen said, "How y'all girls doing?"

"We're fine," they said.

"What brings y'all by?" Mrs. Helen asked.

"Mrs. Helen, I'm getting married soon. We came to see if you could do the flowers for my wedding," Anita said.

Mrs. Helen jumped up and said, "Wait right here, I'll be right back!"

Mrs. Helen ran into her house and came back out with a big book. She sat back down and put the book on her lap. Then she said, "Now we can talk. What kind of flowers are you having at the wedding? What type of bouquet are you going to carry? Are the men wearing boutonnieres and the ladies wearing corsages?"

"Yes ma'am, but I don't know what kind!" Anita said.

"That's why I ran into the house to get my book so that y'all can look through it and see what you want," Mrs. Helen stated.

She passed the book to Anita and said, "Look through the book and see what you like. Go on, take your time."

While flipping through the pages, they started saying words like, "Ooh. Ahh. That's pretty. Oh, I like that one. That's nice."

Then Henri, Anita's mom, said, "Helen, what's the cost for the flowers and everything that needs to be done?"

"Well, it depends on the kind of flowers you want; some flowers have to be ordered. That could run you way up. What kind do you have in mind?" Helen asked.

"We are looking now; they are all beautiful. Give us a minute," Henri said.

Anita said, "I love the lilies. The Calla lilies and the Birds of Paradise are the flowers I want. I want one of the lilies for the men, the ring bearer, the ladies, and the flower girl. My bouquet and the maid of honor's may have to have other flowers added to it. If so, I don't mind as long as the two main flowers are seen on the bouquet."

"Baby, I can make whatever you want. I am here to please my customers," Mrs. Helen said.

"Ok, so Helen, now that we know that we are working with the lily family and whatever else that's going into the bouquet, we will need five flowers for the men and two flowers for the mothers," Henri said.

Then Leslie said, "Henri, let's get it straight. You counted wrong; you left out a few people. Let's name them. Now for the men, you have the pastor, the groom, Mr. Blackmon, the two dads, the best man, and the ring bearer, that's seven. And for the ladies, you have the pastor's wife, Mrs. Blackmon, the two moms, the maid of honor, and the flower girl, so that makes six, not including the bouquet, so that's a total of thirteen. You counted seven total; somebody was going to be short."

And then Leslie said, "Helen, we have not set a date yet, but we do know what you have to do will take some time, so we will call you this week. We have to run into town and get the fabric so we can start making what we are going to wear!"

Helen said, "Y'all don't mind if I come along? I have to buy ribbon and some things to make these flowers. By the way, what colors are you having in the wedding, Nita?"

Anita said, "Oh, I'm sorry, Mrs. Helen. It's silver and gold."

"That will be real beautiful," Helen said.

"No, Helen, we don't mind if you come along," Henri said.

"Well let me go grab my purse and take this apron off. I'll be right back," Helen said.

Helen went into the house. The ladies walked to the car and got in to wait for her.

All of the ladies were excited. Helen knew that she was getting ready to make some money and the ladies knew that they were getting ready to be the talk of the town, so they wanted to give them something to talk about.

They pulled up on the lot of the shopping mall and parked the car. Henri said, "Come on, girls. We got work to do. Ain't no time to shuck and jive."

Anita said, "You got that right. I don't know about the men wanting to wear their old suits, even though they still look good in them. But one thing I do know is, the ladies, oh, we are going to be sharp."

They got out of the car, went into the store, and started looking around. Henri and Anita went over to the pattern books to find the gown that they liked, while Helen went over to the flowers. Anita had the picture of the gown that she wanted to wear, so she looked at the fabric and the ribbons, trying to find the right silver and gold prints for the trim on her gown and the flower girl's gown.

The ladies were having a very hard time trying to decide on the pattern, the fabric, and the ribbons, because there was so much to choose from. They were a little undecided; now on the other hand, Mrs. Helen found what she needed. She put the materials in her basket, took them up to the counter, and paid for them. Then she sat down and waited on the rest of them to make up their minds.

After waiting for more than two hours, Mrs. Helen decided to get something to eat, so she got up and left the store. She ordered her food, sat down, and ate it. While she was walking back to the store, she said to herself, "Now I know they have to be ready by now. Ain't that much deciding in the world, either you like it or you don't."

Helen walked back into the store and she could see Nita, Henri, and Leslie still in the same section. After she sat for a few minutes, she said to herself, "Oh no, let me say something; this is getting ridiculous." Then she cleared her throat and made an ugly face. She opened her mouth and said, "We have been at this for over four hours. You could have been sewing something by now. If you can't find everything you need today, get what you have, start with that, and then come back. The way y'all are going the baby will be here and going to school by the time you make up y'all's mind. Yes, I said baby, but so what? Come on, I have flowers to make."

The ladies got a giggle out of Mrs. Helen, and then Nita said, "Did y'all hear what she said about the baby? How did she know?"

Leslie said, "Girl, Helen is older than all three of us. She's seen a lot of girls leave town and come back later with babies. Not too many of them got married. Don't worry about Helen, she is not one that runs her mouth."

"Well, she just ran it, and she wants us to hurry up. Can you believe she's rushing us? Don't she know we want to look real nice for the wedding? And on top of that, she's riding with us!" Henri said.

"Yes, Henri. She knows. But we have been in this store for a long time. Have we decided on everything? Do we have all that we need, like the zippers, the thread, the elastic, the lining, and whatever else we need? It's past my lunchtime now," Leslie said.

"I think we do, and if we have to come back, we will. So let's head to the checkout," said Henri.

As they walked towards the checkout counter, Helen said, "Y'all sure you got what you need? I thought you were going to buy the whole store."

Leslie said, "Well if we don't, we have a good start. We are going to go home and get started. This is going to take some time."

"I know it will. From what I see, it's going to be beautiful," Helen said.

"Yes, it is," Nita replied.

It has been three weeks since they all went to the fabric store. The ladies started working fast and hard on making what they were going to wear for the wedding and the men as well. Just like the men did when they were building the church, they worked night and day. The ladies did the same with little breaks in between. When they cooked, they prepared very quick and easy meals for their families.

Anita's gown was white; the pattern of her gown looked to be more like a tent style. She did not want a close fit because of her pregnancy bump. It was going to have lace trimmed in silver and gold, the same print as the men's ties and cummerbunds.

Leslie decided on the gold and Henri was going to wear the silver. They both would be wearing gowns. The flower girl would wear a white lace dress below the knee with silver and gold flowers on it.

The men's bow ties, ties, and cummerbunds were made first. The ladies knew that project was easy and it would take no time, so they wanted to get them out of the way.

When Anita's gown was completed, they called her to come try it on. It was a perfect fit and she was very excited.

They called Helen to see how the flowers were coming along.

"Hey, Helen," Leslie said.

Then Helen said, "Hey."

"How are you coming along with the flowers?" Leslie asked.

Helen said, "Don't worry about the flowers, y'all have more to do than what I had to do. I plan to do a good job and that's what I did. Now the flowers are beautiful. If you want, you're welcome to come down and look at them and tell me what you think. How are y'all coming along with all that you two have to make?"

Leslie said, "We are moving right along. We have most of it done. Henri and I have been working so hard we have not taken a break. So I think we will take a break today and come down to see the flowers and then run pass Pearlie's house and look at the cakes. Then we need to run into town and look at some shoes. If I can't find me a pair of nice cheap shoes, then I will wear what I have."

Helen said, "I know that's right. Ain't no need to spend a lot of money!"

But then Leslie said, "Oh believe me, we are going to do everything the cheapest way we can. But it will be a nice wedding, you know what I mean?"

"I know what you mean. Look, I got food on the stove, I'll see you when you come down," Helen said.

After their called ended, Henri said, "What day do you think we should set the wedding for?"

Leslie said, "First, we have to make sure Pastor Penny can do the day we set. We have to make sure everything is ready to go, like the food. I know they took Chuck-Chuck to the slaughterhouse two weeks ago, so that's taken care of. We have to send the kids out in the garden to do a lot of picking. Then we have to ask for help with the cooking. Let's talk with the pastor on Sunday and see what dates are best for him, and then we will have it announced in service. Now let's take a break and run down to Helen's house."

So the ladies paused for a break. They moved any obstructions out of the way, grabbed their purses, and went out the door. Henri, Anita, and Leslie got into the car and headed down the road to Helen's house.

When they pulled in front of her house, just like they usually do, they tooted the horn and yelled out of the window.

"Hey, Helen," Leslie yelled. Like always, Helen was sitting on the porch, swaying back and forth on her rocking bench.

Helen yelled back, "Y'all come on in the house. Let me show you the flowers; they are beautiful, if I must say so myself."

So they got out of the car and walked towards Helen's house. They opened the gate, went into the yard, and walked up the two steps into the house.

Helen said, "Come sit down. Let me go grab the box. I'll be right back."

Helen came back with the box that had the flowers in it. She sat the box down on the coffee table. Henri, Leslie, and Anita started to pick up the flowers from the box.

Anita said, "These are so beautiful."

Helen said, "Thank you, Nita. I'm glad you like them."

Then Nita said, "Like them? I love them; they are really pretty."

And then Henri said, "Helen, you outdid yourself. I love these; they are so gorgeous. How much are you charging for them?"

"Well, Henri, what I paid for the materials and the time it took me. Since we are neighbors and friends, $75.00 for you!" Helen said.

"I am glad we put money away for a rainy day; you never know what might come along and you need emergency money. Thanks, Helen," Henri said.

Henri reached down into her purse and pulled out the money. She handed it to her and said, "Helen, I thank you so much. I don't know what we would have done without you. If we had to go to the florist to have the flowers done, I know we would have paid a lot more; I owe you."

Anita stood up, picked up the box of flowers, and looked at Henri and Les, with gesture and said, "We have other things to take care of, so let's go."

"Don't y'all have to go to Pearlie's house to check on the cake? I'm not rushing y'all, but this is my naptime," Helen said.

Leslie replied by saying, "Yes, we'd better be running along. We still have to go into town. Let's go y'all."

They left Helen's and headed to Pearlie's house. Pearlie lived on the other side of the railroad tracks, so they had to drive up the road for a short distance, then cross over the tracks. They reached Pearlie's house, parked, got out of the car, and went into the house. As the screen door closed, Pearlie said, "Who that is?"

Henri said, "It's me, Les, and Nita."

"Come on back, I'm in the kitchen baking a cake for Agnes's birthday," Pearlie said.

So they walked back towards the kitchen, smelling the aroma of cake baking. When they reached the kitchen, Pearlie said, "I was wondering when you all were going to come over so that you can choose the cake you want."

Pearlie pulled out her book of cake designs and they sat down at the table to look at the different cakes.

They knew that they would need to have either a very big cake or multiple cakes so that everyone would get a slice. They didn't have a headcount because the wedding will be announced during Sunday service and they were also thinking about family that lived out of town.

What they decided on were two whole sheet cakes and a half sheet cake with layers.

Pearlie said to Anita, "Have you decided on the kind of cake?"

Anita said, "I love chocolate and vanilla, but my family loves lemon. So I think we can have the two sheet cakes on the side, one made with lemon mix and yellow icing, and the other made with white mix and lemon icing, and the wedding cake can be chocolate and another kind of icing that would look pretty and match the colors of the wedding."

Then Pearlie said, "I would have to experiment with my food coloring and see how close I can come to the colors that you have chosen. Silver and gold is the talk around town. I think that would look real nice; I can do it."

Anita smiled and said, "Thanks so much, Cousin Pearlie."

"Pearlie, besides the ingredients, what else would you need?" Henri asked.

"Nothing. You gave me that big bag of flour sitting over there, the chocolate powder, the wax paper, and the food coloring. I have plenty of lard. We don't need eggs. I can't think of anything else, but if something comes up that I don't have, I will call you," Pearlie said.

"Pearlie, I thank you, but we'd better run. We have to go into town and try to find some cheap shoes and then get back to the house so that we can finish these gowns. We are almost done. Will I see you at church tomorrow?" Henri said.

Pearlie said, "If the Lord is willing and the creek don't rise, I will be in the church house with my shouting shoes on."

The three of them got up and headed towards the front door, and Leslie said, "Thanks again, Pearlie, I'll see you tomorrow in church."

When they got into the car, Anita said, "Who's going to take the pictures?"

Leslie said, "Everybody who has a camera will be taking pictures. We can have Bubba to be the photographer. You know how he wants to be seen."

Henri and Nita laughed. Then Henri said, "I can see him saying, 'I got this, step aside, move a little to the left, step a little to the right, smile.' I can't wait. We are going to hear all of that."

"Now y'all know we are going to have a lot of laughs. Bubba is my brother and we all know he's a mess of a show-off," Les said.

Right after Leslie said that about Bubba, they pulled up beside him sitting at the light, with the windows down in the car.

Leslie said, "I was just talking about you two seconds ago!"

Bubba said, "Oh yeah, what about? I hope it was good."

"It wasn't bad. We need you to take lots of pictures at Aaron and Anita's wedding," Les said.

Bubba said, "Now sis, we haven't talked in a few weeks. When did this all come about?"

Les said, "Come about? Monty said he told you when y'all were working on the church!"

"Oh yeah, that's right, he did. So when is the wedding?" Bubba said.

"We are not sure; we're going to talk with Pastor tomorrow. Right now, we are trying to get everything together before we talk with him. We had to make our clothes. Oh, by the way, can you make some barbeque? We can add that to the menu," Les said.

"Sure, I can," Bubba answered.

Henri said, "Y'all better be glad that this is not a busy road. We sat through three lights. You two running y'all's mouth. Call him on the phone, Les; we got things to do."

Then Leslie said, "I'll talk with you later."

Bubba said, "See y'all later."

Then they drove off. When they pulled into the parking lot, there was a park in front of the shoe store. They saw Pastor and Mrs. Penny, so they tooted the horn, waved, and then they got out of the car.

Pastor Penny said, "Well ladies, how are you three doing today?"

Leslie, Henri, and Nita said, "Hi, Pastor and Mrs. Penny."

"I mentioned your name to Bubba just a few minutes ago," Leslie said.

Pastor Penny said, "Oh, what about?"

"Well, we wanted to get with you to set a date for the wedding, so that we can have it announced in Sunday service," Leslie said.

Then Pastor said, "Ok, let me check my calendar and I can give you a date when I see you at Sunday school. I will see you three in Sunday school, won't I?"

"We will be in Sunday school," Leslie said.

Pastor Penny said, "It's Communion Sunday. We have some new members and we're giving them the right hand of fellowship."

"Mount Anna is really growing. Sisters, we will see you in the morning, and I'll have the dates with me. Good day, ladies," he said.

"I love our pastor," Henri said.

Then Leslie said, "We all love him. He brings forth the Word."

The ladies walked into the store where there was a big 50% off sale sign on the window.

Anita said, "I hope we can find something that will go with what we're wearing."

"We sure are spending money like it's not hard to come by. I am so glad we know how to bargain shop," Henri said.

Leslie said, "Yes, I am."

When the ladies started looking at the shoes, one of the sales associates came up to them and said, "We have a big sale today."

Henri said, "Yes, we saw the sign on the window."

"Oh, no ma'am, we also have buy two pairs of shoes and get the third pair free," the sales associate said.

"Free," with a high-pitched voice," Henrietta said.

With that awesome sale, the ladies shopped and bought shoes for everyone in the wedding party, and they paid less than $100.

The ladies carried the bags to the car, happy knowing that they got a steal.

Leslie said, "I hope we got the right size for everyone, like the maid of honor and the best man."

Anita said, "We did. Corky wears the same size shoes as me, and Dwayne wears the same size as Aaron; so we are set."

"Good," Leslie said.

"Now that we have most of the sewing completed, we are going to do the final fittings tomorrow, finish the hemming, and then the hard part comes. Henri, we have to call around to see who is willing to help us with all the food we have to prepare," Leslie said.

When Sunday came, it was time to rise and shine and give God the glory. As the people in the small town got ready for church, Anita, Leslie, and Henrietta were anxious to hear what dates Pastor Penny will have available for the wedding day; they couldn't wait to get to church.

As they left the house and headed to the church house, Anita and her family and Aaron and his family walked swiftly to the church, ready to hear what date Pastor Penny could perform their wedding.

Most of the people in the small town who could walk would walk to church. While on the way to church, families, neighbors, and friends would meet up with each other. They looked forward to being fed for the week, so going to Sunday school and then morning worship were the ways to feast on God's Word.

As the Jacksons and the Wallers walked through the doors of the church, Pastor Penny was standing right there. He greeted all of them by saying, "Good morning, Brother and Sister Jackson, Brother Aaron, little Lisa, Melanie, Karen, master Lamont Jr., and Michael."

Then Pastor greeted the Wallers and said, "Good morning, Brother and Sister Waller, Sister Anita, little Andreya, master Von, Samuel, and Preston. Now that I covered both families, how's everyone this morning?"

They all answered and said, "Good morning, Pastor Penny, we're fine."

Pastor Penny said, "Wonderful, we're having breakfast after Sunday school. Children, if you would go on over to the children's church, I'd like to talk with the adults for a minute."

"If you would, come into my office. We only have a few minutes before Sunday school starts," Pastor said.

"Have a seat," Pastor Penny said, as he walked behind his desk and sat down. "I've looked over my calendar for this month. Next Saturday, I have an engagement. But I am available to perform the wedding ceremony on the third and the fourth Saturdays. I don't know how soon you want the date to be. If it's next month, I have no engagements."

They all looked at each other, then Leslie said, "We have done everything we need to do, except the cooking. We can call family and friends to let them know. What about the last Saturday of this month?

All agree, raise your hand."

They all raised their hands.

"Good. Well Pastor, it looks like our children will be getting married on the last Saturday of this month. Thank you, Pastor Penny," Leslie said.

Pastor Penny smiled, as Aaron and Anita jumped up and hugged each other.

Then Pastor said, "Brother Aaron and Sister Anita, I would like to meet with both of you for marriage counseling on Friday of this week and the following Saturday at 6:30, for a few hours, and then Friday before the wedding rehearsal."

Anita said, "Yes, Pastor Penny."

Aaron said, "We will be here, sir, thank you."

Pastor looked at his watch and said, "Oh my, we have two minutes before Sunday school starts. I will have the secretary to announce the wedding date during the announcements. Any questions?"

They all said, "No questions, Pastor, thank you."

They walked out of the pastor's study and headed to the room where Sunday school was being held.

After having breakfast, morning worship began. Like always, when the time came for the announcements, Mrs. Ruby, the clerk, read all that was going to take place.

Then she said, "Congratulations are in order. Brother Aaron Jackson will be marrying Sister Anita Waller on the last Saturday of this month, August 26th. All are invited."

Then Mrs. Ruby looked at the pastor and said, "What time?"

Then he looked out into the congregation and he saw Lamont, Aaron's dad, hold up one finger. He then told Mrs. Ruby, "I was just informed,

1 o'clock in the afternoon."

Mrs. Ruby then said, "The wedding will be held at 1:00 in the afternoon on Saturday, August 26th. Be sure to mark your calendars, thank you."

As Mrs. Ruby walked to her seat, Pastor Penny got up and said, "Congratulations are in order. Now that the final touch-ups were completed in the church, looks like we will have the first wedding in our new sanctuary. Let's give Sister Anita and Brother Aaron a hand. There's no doubt that they love one another. Congratulations!"

Then Pastor Penny turned, walked, and took his seat. It was offering time, so the deacons came forth. As the music played and the choir sang, the congregation came to bring their tithes and offerings. Altar prayer was next; that was for anyone who needed a blessing or to just give thanks to our Heavenly Father. Then the choir sang a few selections, and after that, Pastor Penny brought forth the Word from the Lord.

After service was over, many people came up to Aaron and Anita to congratulate them.

Henri said, "If anyone wants to help us with preparing the food, call me. We only have three weeks to put this all together, thank you."

Time passed by so swiftly. On August 25th, which was the day of the wedding rehearsal, Aaron and Anita had to meet with Pastor Penny for their last counseling session before the rehearsal started. Meanwhile, the wedding party, family, and friends were decorating the sanctuary and outside.

The rehearsal went well with no problems, but they were all tired from preparing the food for tomorrow.

August 26th was the day that Aaron and Anita were becoming one. Family came from out of town. The men got up early to take most of the food to the church, along with lots of wood for the barbeque pits.

Some of the friends that offered to help were staying at the church to cook and add the finishing touches to whatever was needed.

The wedding party agreed that they would all meet at the church one hour before the ceremony began.

The men and women ushers of the church offered to help. They would be responsible for pinning the corsages and boutonnieres on and ushering the guests down to their seats. The bride's family and friends were going to be seated on one side, and the groom's family and friends were going to be on the opposite side. The ushers were also going to pass out the programs and offer to take the gifts for the couple. There was a table set up outside for the gifts and a decorated box in the middle for the cards. They were also going to give everyone a small wrapping filled with rice to throw at the bride and groom after the ceremony was over.

At eleven fifteen in the morning, people started to come into the church. Some had gift boxes and some had cards.

It was a tradition that the bride and groom should not see each other before the wedding, so they agreed that one family would go to the church one-half hour before the other. The Wallers planned to arrive at the church by 12:00 noon, and the Jacksons were due to arrive at 12:30. They agreed to be in separate rooms until it was time for the ceremony to start. If there were any last-minute preparations, it would have to be done in the waiting room.

Brother and Sister Blackmon coordinated everything. Mrs. Blackmon was going to be in the room with the ladies. Her job was to direct them and let them know when they were to enter the sanctuary. She would allow them the distance space between each person in the wedding party as they walked down the aisle. She coached the flower girl again on what she needed to do and she also made sure everything and everyone looked stunning before the wedding started.

Mr. Blackmon was going to be in the room with the men, making sure little Michael, the ring bearer, would hold the pillow the correct way. Mr. Blackmon made sure that the men looked real sharp and he directed them as they entered the sanctuary.

It was now getting close to the time for the Wallers to be heading to the church.

Bubba arrived early with lots of film and a few cameras that all hung around his neck. He walked around taking pictures of everything and every guest that entered into the church. He went outside to take pictures of the setup and of the people who were helping outside.

Anita and her family arrived at the church and they went into their assigned rooms. They were happy but nervous. They remained in the room until the start of the wedding. Mrs. Blackmon looked at the ladies and said, "You all look so beautiful, and Sister Anita, you are a gorgeous bride."

Nita responded by saying, "Thank you, Mrs. Blackmon."

Then Mrs. Blackmon said, "While we wait for Sister Jackson, I am going to work with little Miss Andreya on how to hold her basket and throw the flower pieces. When the Jacksons arrive, the ushers will come and pin on the corsages and boutonnieres. Pastor and First Lady Penny will come in and give a quick prayer, and after that, I'll instruct you on what's next!"

While Mrs. Blackmon worked with Andreya, she told her, "I think you will be one of the best flower girls Aiken, South Carolina, has seen yet. You did very well. Now, when you get in front of all the guests, I want you to do even better."

Andreya shook her head and said, "Yes ma'am, I will."

"Now give me a hug, baby girl," Mrs. Blackmon said.

The groom and his family arrived at the church. Mr. Blackmon stood outside waiting for them. He waved his hand as to say, "Come on, hurry up."

They got out of the car. Mr. Blackmon said, "Come on, we only have 30 minutes, and I have to make sure everything is right, especially with my little man who is going to be carrying the rings."

Mr. Blackmon put his hand out and shook all of the men's hands, and he said to Michael, "Come on, little fella. Let's see how you are going to carry the pillow. All the men are in this meeting room right here."

So now the entire wedding party had arrived at the church. Pastor Penny walked into the room where the men were, along with Sister Sandra, one of the ushers. She was pinning on the men's boutonnieres.

After she was done, the pastor said, "Let me give a quick prayer. Shall we bow our heads? Oh Gracious Father, we come before you on this day that you have made, giving thanks for this young man, your son, Aaron, who is marrying at a young age. God he's stepping up. I pray that this union will grow to become a blessing for many, in Jesus' name I pray, Amen."

"Now let me go down the hall where the ladies are. First, let me say, you men look mighty sharp. I'll see you in the sanctuary," Pastor Penny said.

Pastor Penny turned to walk out the room and Sister Sandra walked out behind him. She stopped and said, with a smile on her face, "Y'all look real nice."

Mr. Blackmon said to young Michael as he handed him the pillow, "Ok, fella, I know you remember what we practiced last night when you carried the pillow."

Young Michael said, "Yes sir, I remember. Do you want me to show you what we did?"

Mr. Blackmon was shocked. He said, "Yes, show me how you are going to walk while you are carrying the pillow with the rings on it."

Young Michael walked over to a corner. He held his head up and put the pillow waist high. With his hands under the pillow and with a smile on his face, he walked towards the men who were standing on the opposite side of the room.

They clapped their hands and said, "Alright boy, you got it."

Michael smiled and said, "Thank you."

Pastor Penny and Sister Sandra were now at the room where the ladies were. He knocked on the door and someone inside said, "Come in."

They went into the room with both of their eyes stretched wide. The ladies laughed and Leslie said, "If you could only see your faces."

Then Sister Sandra said, "We just left the room with the men and I told them how nice they looked. Then we come down here, you ladies look so beautiful. Look at the bride. Nita, you are gorgeous, let me give you your bouquet; and Corky, here's yours, and let's pin on the corsages."

"I don't think I could have said it any better. Ladies, you all look nice," Pastor Penny said.

While Sister Sandra pinned on the corsages, Leslie said, "Who is that singing? They have been really doing it up."

Pastor said, "That's Brother Andrew and Sister Loretta."

"Well, they better save their voices, because they have to sing as we walk down the aisle." Just when Leslie said that, the singing stopped.

Pastor said, "You see, Sister Jackson, God is in control! Now we only have ten minutes. I'm going to have a short word of prayer before we start. Shall we pray? With all hearts clear, Eternal and all wise, Father God, we come on behalf of these two families praying that you would keep them in your loving care. Not only the bride and groom, but all of them as a whole. Just as you have always done, in Jesus' name we pray, Amen."

"Sister Blackmon, are we ready?" Pastor Penny asked.

"Yes, Pastor. We are," she said.

"It's time for First Lady Penny and I to be escorted into the sanctuary," he said.

Bubba was in position; he had reloaded his camera a few times.

The pastor and his wife walked out of the room and two ushers were standing in the hall. There was a lady usher for Pastor Penny and a male usher for First Lady Penny.

As Brother Andrew sang, *"You Are So Beautiful,"* the pastor and his wife were being escorted down the aisle by the ushers.

Then Lamont escorted Henri down the aisle to her seat on the front pew and he walked back up the aisle to escort his wife to their seats on the front pew.

After the parents were seated, Mr. Blackmon told Aaron, "Sister Linda and Sister Hazel are standing in the hallway waiting to usher you and Dwayne down."

As Sister Linda and Sister Hazel stood in service position with one arm behind their back and their fist in the center of the back, wearing their white gloves, Aaron and Dwayne came out of the room. The ushers made a sharp turn as they walked in front of Aaron and Dwayne down the aisle. When they got closer to the front of the church, both ushers stepped aside and greeted Aaron and Dwayne, by holding out one hand to direct them as they walked over to where they will stand.

Mr. Blackmon told Michael, "Ok fella, it's time for you to walk down the aisle."

Michael said, "Yes sir, I'm ready."

"Ok, you can start now," Mr. Blackmon stated.

Then master Michael began walking down the aisle with a big smile on his face. As he got closer, someone yelled, "Awesome job, little Mike." That really made him step even better. He reached the front and stood next to the best man.

Mr. Blackmon walked down the hall, knocked on the door, and talked at the same time, "Ok ladies, the usher is here to usher Corky down the aisle."

Mrs. Blackmon opened the door and said, "Ok, we are ready."

Milton stood in position, ready to escort Corky down the aisle. She came out of the room and took him by the arm. As they walked down the aisle, at the halfway point, they stopped. He bowed and she curtseyed. Then Corky walked down to the front where she had to stand.

Then two ushers came to roll out the runner all the way down to the front of the church. When they walked back up the aisle, that's when Mrs. Blackmon gave directions to Andreya.

"Ok, baby girl, it's your time now. Do a good job!" she said.

When Andreya came into the sanctuary, the two ushers closed the doors and stood in front of them. While Andreya walked down the aisle, she did a perfect job. With a smile on her face, she stood next to the maid of honor.

When Andreya reached the front of the church, that was when Brother Andrew stopped singing, and then Pastor Penny said, "All rise."

Everyone in the congregation stood up and started looking towards the back of the church. The organist started playing, *"Here Comes the Bride."* That's when the ushers opened up the doors, and all you could hear was, "Ooh."

As Anita and her dad walked down the aisle, what a beautiful sight was that to see. Tears were in so many eyes.

Mr. and Mrs. Blackmon walked in and sat in the rear of the church.

When Anita and her dad reached the front of the church, they stood in front of Pastor Penny. Pastor Penny then told everyone, "You may be seated." Then he said, "Good afternoon everyone, on this glorious beautiful day that the Lord has made. We gather here today in our new sanctuary, giving thanks to our All Mighty God, for blessing this young man and this young lady in holy matrimony. Who gives this young lady away?"

Ail, Anita's dad, said, "I do."

After he gave his daughter away, he turned towards Anita, hugged her, and said, "I love you."

Anita smiled and said, "I love you too, Daddy." Then he turned and walked to take his seat next to his wife. Then Aaron stood next to Anita.

The pastor went on to perform the ceremony. The couple said their vows, then Brother Ellis sang the Lord's Prayer, and Aaron saluted his bride with a kiss.

Then the family and guests stood up and clapped as the wedding party walked out of the sanctuary.

An announcement was made that the wedding party would return into the sanctuary to take pictures. The guests were welcomed to stay and watch or they could go outside for refreshments.

After taking pictures, the wedding party stood inside to be announced before going outside to greet the guests.

With all the excitement going on, the wedding party finally took their seat at the bridal party table, so now they could see what was going on around them.

A large number of people came out to show love and support. There were friends from elementary school that moved away, family they hadn't seen in years, all came back to celebrate with them.

The bride and her dad danced, the bride and groom danced, and whoever else wanted to dance did. They just had a good ole time.

There was an outpour of love from the church family. The ushers put on their aprons to help serve the food and drinks.

The cakes were beautiful. Pictures were taken as the couple cut the cake.

Later, after everything was over, whoever was left pitched in to help clean up.

Their parents gave them a key to a room at the town's hotel, and that's where they spent their wedding night. They spent most of the night opening cards. When they saw that money was in them, they did not stop until all the cards were opened and read. The money that was given to them was over four thousand dollars, and that was a total shock. They both laughed and cried. They decided to give their duplicate gifts as Christmas gifts and keep what they needed for their own place.

Patsy and her family planned to use this vacation time for their trip to Disney World. All the children were going along with them. The days they planned to spend in Florida would allow Anita and Aaron to start packing their things for their move to D.C., so they could start a new life. They were going to live in the basement apartment of Chris and Patsy's house.

With all the excitement, the bride and groom stayed up most of the night, then they later rolled over and went to sleep.

When Anita and Aaron finally woke up around noon the next day, both of them wanted to stay at the hotel for another day. So they took a small portion of their gift money and paid for another day's stay.

When the newlyweds checked out of the hotel, they went to Aaron's house. He wanted to tell his parents his plans about his move to D.C. with Anita to find a job and enroll into school.

When Anita and Aaron walked into the house, his parents were sitting in the living room. His mom said with a smile on her face, "Well, good morning, newlyweds."

They both replied by saying, "Good morning."

Aaron's dad said, "Come on and have a seat. We were just talking about how beautiful the wedding and the reception were. We are proud of you two."

Aaron said, "Thanks Daddy. You know, Anita and I were talking. She's going back with Chris and Patsy. I feel it would not be right if I let my wife, who is carrying my baby, go 800 miles away, when I should be with her. So I think it's best that I go along with them and enroll into one of the schools there and find a job. That way we both can go to school, work, and save some money."

"Good idea, son. I knew you would be a responsible husband. Just like I know my parents did not raise a fool and neither did I. You know if you need me or your mom, we will be a phone call away. I am glad that you two will be starting a new life together," Lamont said.

STARTING A NEW LIFE TOGETHER

Chapter Four

After Anita and Aaron got married, they felt a lot better knowing that they were starting a new life together as husband and wife, even if they were living in the basement of Patsy's home. They knew that this was not their dream home, but it was their home for now, while they work, save money, raise their baby, and go to school.

They did not lay around; Aaron and Anita were on a mission. They arrived at Patsy's house around 2 o'clock in the morning. They unloaded everything from the vehicle and carried it into the house.

After the last load, Aaron said, "Nita, where is the bag that has our night clothes, soap, toothbrushes, and all that kind of stuff?"

Anita said, "It's right here," as she held the bag up.

"Ok, good. I don't want to mix it up with everything else. That's all we need right now. When we get up in the morning, we have a lot to do, so let's get ready for bed," he said.

Lights out!

When they woke up, Anita said to Aaron, "Good morning, husband, so, how are we going to attack this day?"

Aaron's reply was, "Well, good morning to you, my wife. I think we need to go over to Howard University first, since it's closer to us and try to enroll there. After that, we can apply for some jobs around the neighborhood. We need to open up an account at the bank. Then when we get back here we can start putting our stuff away; this is a mess right now. What do you think?"

Anita said, "Sounds good to me; let's do it."

The basement of Patsy's house was designed into an apartment with its own entrance.

The newlyweds got up, showered, and got dressed. Then they went upstairs. Chris, Patsy's husband, was sitting in the kitchen drinking coffee. He said, "Good morning, how did y'all sleep?"

Aaron and Anita both said, "We slept hard as a rock."

Then Aaron said, "It wasn't long enough, but we have a lot to do today, so we are getting an early start."

Then Chris said, "Well, you know the area; it's not like this is your first time in the city. If I can help in any way, let me know. Oh, by the way, Pat is still sleeping and help yourself to the kitchen. Eat something before you leave the house."

Anita said, "Thanks, Uncle Chris."

Then Aaron said "Uncle Chris, you know I want to study law, and you and Aunt Pat know lots of lawyers. Can you see if any of them need any help? I want to get my foot in the door."

Chris said, "Sure, I will call a few of them today. So what are your plans for today?"

Anita said, "We are going over to the university and try to enroll there. Then we are going to look for jobs. And then we are going to open up a bank account. And after that, we are going to come back and start putting our things away."

"So Uncle Chris, after we are done with our running around today, do you mind taking us to the grocery store? We need to buy some food," Aaron said.

"Man, all this food we brought for the trip that didn't get eaten, it's like we just took it along with us. The children wanted to eat out all the time. Please help us eat this stuff up first, then after it's all gone, I won't mind taking you, ok?" Chris said.

Aaron said, "Ok, thanks."

When Anita started to prepare something for breakfast, she cooked enough for everyone in the house, and she said, "Uncle Chris, when everyone gets up, all they have to do is warm the food up."

Chris said, "Thanks, Nita. I was going to cook breakfast, but I thank you for doing it."

So the three of them ate while the food was hot, and Chris said, "I'll wash the dishes. I know you want to get an early start."

"Are you sure?" Aaron said. "We don't mind washing the dishes."

Chris said, "Oh, I got this. You will have plenty of days washing and cleaning. Don't worry, I got it."

"So I hear after you two graduate from college, your parents are going to let you live in the home in Florida to raise your family. You ready for that?" Chris asked.

Aaron said, "Well, when the time comes, we'll be ready. Right now, we want to save money and see what happens later."

Aaron and Anita finished breakfast. Anita said, "Uncle Chris, we are off to start our day. Pray that all goes well, and tell Aunt Patsy we will see her later. Thanks again for letting us stay here."

Chris said, "It's already done. Trust and believe, much success will happen for both of you today, and I'll tell your auntie. Oh, before you go Aaron, after you enroll in school, go by Gillis and Bright Law Firm. Their office is located on the same side of the street as the university. You would go up about four blocks. When you go into the office, ask for Reginald Gillis or Larry Bright. They are both buddies of mine and I know they will help me out. I'm going to give them a call. They will be expecting your visit."

Aaron said, "Gee thanks, Uncle Chris, I owe you."

Then he looked at Anita, with a smile on his face, and said, "Things are looking up, Praise God."

So they turned and walked out the door.

Aaron did get a job at the Law Firm of Gillis and Bright. He was happy about that. Anita also was hired at Howard University Hospital. They both had jobs and they passed the entrance exam for Howard University. This turned out to be a blessing for the both of them.

After they completed those two tasks, they went to the bank to open up a savings account and a checking account in both their names. Things did go according to plan. After all of their tasks were completed, despite having one of Chris and Patsy's cars to drive, they decided to just walk around the neighborhood.

Any extra money needed while Aaron and Anita went to school and worked their part-time jobs, the financial help came from the family.

The Jacksons and the Wallers were not family by blood, but only by marriage. The love and trust they shared with each other made their relationship feel like they were family.

It was now November and Thanksgiving was in one week. The Jacksons and the Wallers all prepared to come up for the

Thanksgiving holiday. They were hoping that their grandbaby, who was due to come around that time, would come, because their plan was to stay longer.

When the parents and children arrived at Patsy's house, Anita's mom walked over to the basement door and started yelling down the stairs.

"Henri's here. Y'all come up. Let me see how the baby has grown. Come, give us a hug," then she walked over to the couch and sat down.

They were going to check into a hotel, but Patsy was not standing for that, so they all stayed with Patsy and her family. The sleeping arrangements were tight, but it worked out. The boys slept in Spencer's room and the girls shared a room with Dallas. Alfred and Henri Waller slept in the guest bedroom. Lamont and Leslie Jackson slept in the office, but they didn't mind. They were all happy to be together.

The newlyweds came upstairs. They all ran to each other, giving kisses and hugs.

Henri said, "Girl, you think the baby will wait until after Thanksgiving? Looks like that little one is ready to come out now. How are you feeling?"

Anita said, "I feel good; I have no problems at all!"

On Tuesday, they planned the menu for the Thanksgiving dinner. The ladies said they would do the grocery shopping.

They all agreed on the menu. The men didn't care what they ate as long as it was good. Henri wanted Anita to go shopping with them so that she could walk. She was so anxious to see her grandbaby. She felt if Nita walked, hopefully this would bring the baby down. But Anita said, "I walk all the time. The baby is not going to come until he or she is ready. You know that!"

Anita's dad looked at her and said, "Girl, I think that baby is going to come real soon. You look like you are ready to pop. You sure are sticking out there. How do you feel?"

Anita said, "Daddy, I feel fine. The baby is due to come around the end of this month, so we will see what happens."

On November 23rd, the day before Thanksgiving, all the ladies were in the kitchen preparing what they could, while the men talked about the football game that would be shown on Thanksgiving Day. The ladies, however, were paying the guys no attention.

They were baking pies, making cakes, and getting the turkey ready for the oven, which was going in last before bed. They had the greens and the string beans on the stove. They cut up fruit for the fruit salad, boiled eggs to make deviled eggs, and cooked whatever else they could cook that night. Tomorrow, they would cook the chicken, roast, ham, macaroni and cheese, the dressing, and the rolls.

Whoever was the last one to go to bed had to put the turkey in the oven, set the timer, and bake it on a low temperature. That way when they get up in the morning, the bird will already be done.

Rise and shine!

Leslie's awake. She got up, took her shower, and started fixing breakfast. Chris came down the stairs and into the kitchen. "Good morning, Les," he said. "I didn't think many of my family members got up as early as me. But, I see I was wrong."

Leslie said, "Morning, I have to get my day started. Believe me, when they start smelling my cooking, they will all get up. Watch what I tell you. I've got the ham and the roast in the oven. I'm letting the rolls rise, which will be a while. Do you know that when we went into the store, they had not only Christmas decorations on display, but Valentine's Day was set up too? Just greed, greed, and greedy! Whatever, they just want your money."

"You know it's all about the money and marketing with most businesses. They want to make a profit any way they can," Chris said.

As Leslie cooked breakfast, she said to Chris, "Well, this is November. Who's going to eat stale candy in February? Listen, what did I tell you? I hear some movement upstairs. The nose don't lie. When they smell some good old fashion country cooking, they come running."

"I don't know about all that Les, because I can throw down on the stove myself," Chris said.

Then Leslie said, "Chris, when you cook, you see, that's city cooking. I'm talking about that good ole down home country cooking. You see, a lot of people don't know nothing about that; it's when you put your foot in the pot."

They both got a big laugh out of that. Then Chris said, "Les, I'd like to see you put your foot in that pot of grits. You gonna draw back a nub."

Leslie said, "A nub is right. They might as well cut my foot off because it won't be any more good, burned to the bone."

"You got that right," Chris said.

When Les yelled upstairs, she said, "Time to rise and shine. Wash your face, brush your teeth, and come down and eat." That's when they all started down the steps, one by one, ready to eat, and then Anita and Aaron came upstairs. They all ate breakfast together.

After breakfast, Anita and Aaron went for a long walk. When they returned, she went downstairs and laid down to take a nap. She slept so long, they started eating the Thanksgiving dinner. Aaron went down to wake her up, but she said she was not hungry.

"Are you feeling ok?" he asked.

Anita said, "I feel fine. I'm just sleepy." So she rolled over and Aaron went back upstairs.

Henri said, "Is Nita coming up for dinner?"

Aaron said, "No, she wants to sleep. She said she feels ok."

They all enjoyed Thanksgiving dinner. Anita did not eat any of it. They watched the game, the kids played, and everyone had a good time.

They all pitched in to clean the kitchen and put away the food. When it was time for bed, everyone said good night.

When Aaron went downstairs, he woke Anita up to tell her to get up and put on her pajamas, and she did so.

The next day was Friday the 25th, everyone in the house was sleeping when Anita got up to use the bathroom. When she wiped herself, she saw some blood. But she did not panic, because her doctor, Gary Cooper, explained to her that this was called a bloody show. He told her that this would happen before her labor pain starts.

Anita called her doctor to let him know what she saw. He told her that her labor pains would start soon and asked her how she felt. She told him that she felt fine.

Anita did not wake Aaron because she felt no pain, so she got back in bed and went to sleep.

When she woke up three hours later, she still had no pain. She got up, took a shower, got dressed, and went out the door. At this time, she left out of the basement door. If her Uncle Chris or Leslie were in the kitchen, they would not know that she was gone.

Anita said to herself, "Let me drive to the hospital to see if I am in labor or not. By the time I go and come back, no one will know that I even left the house."

She drove herself to the hospital, having no pain at all. When Anita walked into the hospital and over to the front desk, she said to the receptionist, "Good morning, I am here to see if I am in labor or not."

The next thing Anita knew, someone was coming towards her pushing a wheelchair. The lady stopped and said, "I'll take you up to labor and delivery!"

Anita said, "Oh, I don't need a chair. I can walk!"

The lady said, "No, it's hospital procedure."

So Anita sat in the chair and was wheeled up to labor and delivery.

Once Anita and the orderly reached the labor and delivery floor, Anita was taken into a room. Then a technician came into the room and said, "Hi, I'm Carolyn. I will be the one to see if you are in labor. I need you to undress, put on this gown with the front opened, and lay on this bed."

So Anita undressed and laid on the bed. The technician rolled over some type of monitoring machine with cords and paper hanging from it. She started to place the cords around the different areas of Anita's belly. Once they were connected, she said to Anita, "You are in labor."

Anita looked at Carolyn and said, "I am?"

Then Carolyn said, "Yes, you are. I'll be right back."

The technician turned and walked out of the room. That room had curtains that divided the patients for privacy. While Anita laid there, she could hear other ladies screaming with pain.

Anita said to herself, "Now, I don't know why those ladies are screaming the way that they are, I'm not feeling anything."

Then the technician walked back into the room and Anita said, "Is it ok if I get up and walk around? It's a little boring just laying here."

The technician looked at the tape and said, "No way!"

Then Anita said, "Well, will it be ok if I go to the bathroom to move my bowels?"

The technician looked at the tape again and said, "That's the baby coming!"

Anita stretched her eyes and said, "It is?"

With a soft gentle voice, the technician said, "Can you get out of this bed and get onto that bed?"

The technician pulled another bed right next to the bed that Anita was laying on.

While leaping and talking at the same time, Anita said, "Sure, I can get out of this bed and on that bed."

When Anita got up on the other bed, she said to Carolyn, "Where are we going?"

Carolyn answered, "Into the delivery room."

As soon as Anita was rolled into the delivery room, Dr. Cooper did not have time to prep himself because the baby was coming.

"It's a boy," the doctor said. He looked at Anita and said, "I have never delivered a baby as easy and so quickly as this one. Congratulations, Mrs. Jackson."

Anita was only in the hospital for ten minutes and the baby weighed close to 7 lbs.

Meanwhile, back at Patsy's, Aaron was now awake. He showered and went upstairs. He could hear everyone talking, as he reached the top.

Henri said, "Well, good morning. Where is your bride?"

Aaron said, "I thought she was up here."

Then Leslie said, with a high-pitched voice, "Up here, we haven't seen Nita this morning."

"I wonder where she is," Aaron said. Then he walked over to the window and saw that the car was gone. "Who was downstairs first this morning?"

Chris said, "I was."

"So, you didn't hear Nita? Did she come upstairs?" Aaron asked.

Chris responded by saying, "When I came downstairs, no one was down here but me. Before I took my shower, I heard the water running for a while. So that must have been Nita in the shower and she must have left out of the basement door."

"Well, she did not have to work today and she didn't have a doctor's appointment. Let me call the hospital," Aaron stated.

So Aaron walked over to get the phone; he called Providence Hospital, one of the assigned hospitals Anita's OBGYN works out of. That's where Anita was to give birth. The phone rang and the receptionist answered.

Aaron said, "Good morning, my name is Aaron Jackson and my wife's name is Anita Jackson. Can you tell me if she came into the hospital within the past hour or so?"

The receptionist said, "You said Anita Jackson, correct?"

Aaron said, "Yes."

"Hold one minute," said the receptionist.

When the receptionist came back, she said, "Sir, we do have an Anita Jackson. She's up on the maternity ward, room 219. Would you like me to connect you to that floor?"

Aaron said, "Yes, please."

Then the receptionist said, "We thank you for choosing Providence Hospital, and one moment while I connect you."

While waiting to be connected, Aaron turned and said, "They have an Anita Jackson on the maternity ward. They're connecting me now."

When the person on the ward answered the phone, she said, "Maternity, Nurse Tolson speaking, how may I help you?"

Aaron said, "Good morning, ma'am. My name is Aaron Jackson and my wife's name is Anita Jackson. Our baby is due any day now, and when I woke up she was gone. I need to know if you have Anita Jackson; her birthday is December 6th, 1960."

Nurse Tolson said, "Hold one moment."

Nurse Tolson came right back and said, "Yes sir, we do have your wife Mrs. Jackson here. She's in room 219, but she's sleeping right now."

"I thank you, Nurse Tolson. I'm on my way," Aaron said.

Aaron hung up the phone and told everyone, "Anita is in the hospital.

I've got to get up there."

Henri said, "Wait a minute. We are all going. Let me get my shoes. The older children can look after the younger ones, and all of them can look after each other."

Henri walked over to the stairs and yelled upstairs, "Hey, one of y'all throw me down my shoes."

Then Leslie yelled, "And one of my wigs."

Chris walked over to the stairs and called Dallas, his daughter, and told her, "We are all going over to the hospital. Anita's at the hospital and I need you to make sure you all behave yourselves. We will be back as soon as we can. The hospital's number will be down here on the table."

Dallas said, "Don't worry, Daddy, we will be ok. We know how to act when adults are not around."

Chris said, "And how is that?"

"The same way we should act when adults are around!" she stated.

Chris said, "Thanks, baby girl. We'll be leaving shortly."

So Aaron, Leslie, Henri, Patsy, Lamont, Alfred, and Chris all left the house and headed to the van. While walking, Aaron said, "I'll drive."

"No, I'll drive. Man, you're not going to kill us trying to get to your wife or have the police chasing us to the hospital. Calm down. We'll be there soon," Chris said.

When they arrived at the hospital, Aaron got out of the van before they could even find a parking space on the lot. He ran into the hospital passed the receptionist to the elevators. He pushed the button multiple times very fast.

The receptionist said, as she shook her head, "Sir, you don't have to push the button over and over, one time will bring the elevator to this floor."

When the door opened, Aaron ran onto the elevator and pushed the floor number, then he pushed the close door button multiple times. The door closed and up to the second floor he went.

When the doors opened on the second floor, he got off running. Aaron looked at the sign on the wall, but he still ran in the opposite direction. He ran past the nurses' station, and one nurse said, "Sir, please don't run down the hall."

But he paid that no attention. When he reached the end of the hallway, that's when he realized he was on the wrong side of the building. So he ran back up the hall past the nurses' station and the same nurse said, "Sir, no running in the hall."

When Aaron finally reached room 219, a nurse was in the room showing Anita how to breastfeed the baby.

Aaron gave Anita a kiss and said, "I missed it. I have missed the birth of my first-born child. Nita, why didn't you get me up when you felt your labor pains?"

Anita said, "I didn't have any labor pains, when I came to the hospital. I was only in there for 10 minutes and the baby was ready to come out. It happened so fast."

"Only 10 minutes, what made you come to the hospital?" Aaron asked.

"Well, when I went to the bathroom real early this morning, I wiped myself and saw some blood. I called the doctor. That's when he said that my labor pains are going to start, so I got back in bed and fell asleep. I was feeling fine, no pains at all. So I said to myself, 'Go to the hospital to see if you are in labor.' So I showered, got dressed, and drove here, with no pains at all. I didn't even have time to call you before Aaron Jr. came out," Anita said.

In came Henri, Leslie, Patsy, Ail, Chris, and Monty, moving very swiftly through the door. The receptionist looked up and said, "The elevators are right there." As she pointed to the elevators, she said, "You only have to push the button one time and it will come."

Leslie said, "Is something wrong with the elevator, Miss?"

The receptionist said, "No, there isn't. The young man who came in running through the doors was pushing the button so many times, I had to let him know that the elevator will come with one push and he looks just like the man standing there."

"Well, the man standing there is Mr. Jackson, my husband and the father of the young man who ran through the door," Leslie said.

When Leslie finished what she had to say, she threw her head up, turned around, and said, "Come on, y'all," as she walked towards the elevator.

Leslie was a little heated. When they all got off the elevator, she looked on the wall to see which direction room 219 was. And they all listened to Leslie and went in the wrong direction.

Leslie, Pasty, Henri, Lamont, Chris, and Alfred walked past the nurses' station, and the same nurse said, "Can I help y'all?"

With a salty voice, Leslie said, "No thanks, we're ok."

So they kept walking. But when they got down to the end of the hall, they saw that they also went in the wrong direction.

Then Chris said, with a louder than normal voice, "Les, we should have known not to listen at anything you say when you get upset." Then he looked at everyone and said, "Why did we listen to her?"

Leslie got a little loud and said, "Well, if all y'all know me like that, then why did any of y'all listen to me?"

Then the nurse came down the hall and said, "Quiet please, you are in a hospital."

"And you think we don't know that we are in a hospital? Please Miss, mind your business," Leslie said.

Then Lamont stepped in and said to the nurse, "Sorry ma'am, we came down the wrong hallway and we are leaving this section now."

The nurse said, "Sir, are you looking for the young man who was running through the halls a little while ago? The reason I ask is because he looked just like you."

Monty said, "Yes, we are. Thank you."

As they walked back up the hall, Henri looked at Les and said, "Girl, that wig must be mighty tight on your head. You've had an attitude with everyone. What is wrong with you?"

Leslie said, "You know, I think I might be a little nervous. I'm a grandma, and I wanted to be in the room when the baby was born."

Henri said, "We all wanted to be in the room while our first grandchild was born, but we weren't, not even the daddy. So we have to get over that and go into this room with a better attitude. Put a smile on your face. You looking like you bit into an onion. Smile girl."

Leslie put on a big smile and said, "Room 219, here we are."

She walked into the room first, making a grand entrance, with her arms open wide, strutting like no other. She walked towards Anita, who was laying in the bed, and gave her a kiss on her forehead.

She asked Nita, "How are you feeling, Mommy?"

Anita said, "I'm feeling good. I have no pains. I'm happy."

Then Leslie walked to the other side of the bed where Aaron was sitting and holding the baby.

She said, "Welcome to our family, my first-born grandbaby. Let me wash my hands and put on a robe, so that I can hold my little pumpkin."

While Leslie washed her hands, Lamont said, "Boy, we went through something finding this room."

Aaron said, "So did I. Tell me about it."

"Well, first thing, if I hear another person tell me that we look so much alike today, I'm going to scream. It started with the lady at the desk in the lobby," Lamont said.

Then Aaron said, "I know. Oh, the lady in the lobby, when I was pushing the elevator button many times, she said to me, 'Sir, you don't have to push the button multiple times, just one time and the elevator will come.' She don't know, but I was trying to get to my family real fast!"

"So, what did you do?" Lamont said.

"I kept pushing the button, and when I got off on this floor, I glanced at the room numbers and still ran the wrong way. Then the lady at the nurses' station said, 'Sir, no running in the hall.' When I got to the end of the hall and did not see the room number, I ran back up the hall and she said the same thing, but I ignored her again."

Lamont said, "Well, our story sounds almost the same. We had to deal with both ladies, or should I say your mama dealt with both of them?"

The visit at the hospital was good. Mommy and baby were doing well. They will be discharged in two days.

The ride home from the hospital was a quality ride. They discussed planning a baby shower and who would care for the baby when Aaron and Anita returned to work. Both grandmas said they would stay to help out if the baby was born during the Thanksgiving holiday, and he was.

Things were working out really good for the new parents, both Aaron and Anita were out of school for the holiday. Patsy worked the night shift, so she was home during the day, and Chris worked in the morning. Caring for little Aaron Jr. was a joy for them.

Aaron's and Anita's younger siblings, along with their dads, went back home. The children had to return back to school and their mothers planned to return home in a few weeks.

This close-knit family may not get along all the time, but the love they had for each other built their closeness closer. Whenever one needed help, they all pitched in, so that kept them happy.

Close to seven years later, Aaron and Anita already celebrated receiving their bachelor's degrees. They were close to finishing their master's degrees, and they were glad that they did not put their education on hold.

MORE THAN A BUNDLE

Chapter Five

Graduating again was a good feeling for them as they reminisced on when Anita knew that she was having a baby and went into a panic mode. They laughed about that and said, "Look where God has brought us."

The new parents were still working the jobs in their field of study and were now making more money. Having their degrees allowed them to be placed in higher positions on the job. They both knew that the dreams and goals they shared together that a higher education was needed, so they kept rolling towards getting their master's. Aaron was studying to become a lawyer with a business major, and Anita, a nurse with a major in science. One thing they agreed on was that they didn't want to make the minimum salary; they wanted to be on top.

During the summer, Aaron Jr. spent lots of time down south with his grandparents and other family. He normally came home three weeks before he returned to school.

Aaron Jr. was seven-and-a-half years old. Things hadn't been all that bad for them with the support of family surrounding them.

Chris and Patsy's two children attended private school, along with Aaron Jr. He loved to read and he read really well at his age. The teachers were impressed because he was well above his grade level. His family looked at this little boy in amazement.

When Anita came home, Aaron was helping Junior with his homework.

They both ate dinner. Afterward, Aaron gave Junior his bath and then he took a shower. Anita kissed both of them and they asked her how her day went. She told them that her day was busy and a little rough.

Aaron prepared dinner, the only thing Anita had to do was wash her hands and sit at the table. While Anita ate her dinner, they all discussed how their day went.

Then Aaron stared at Anita with a puzzled look on his face.

Anita said, "Why are you looking at me that way?"

Aaron said, "I'll talk about it after you eat and shower; it's nothing we need to discuss now."

When Junior was tucked into bed for the night, Aaron and Anita laid in bed watching TV and talking.

Aaron said to Anita, "Is there something you want to tell me?"

Anita looked puzzled and said, "No, tell you about what?"

Then Aaron said, "I think we are going to have another baby and I say that because I feel the same way I did when you were pregnant with Junior."

Then Anita said, "You know, I've started feeling funny too, but 'I'm not pregnant is what I said to myself.' But before I said anything to you, I wanted to be sure. My cycle still comes, but I made an appointment with the doctor. It's tomorrow."

"What time is your appointment? Maybe I can come with you," Aaron said.

"It's at 10:30, which gives me time before I start working. But I think it's a false alarm," Anita said.

"Well, I am coming with you. If I have to go to work late, it will be ok. I don't have court, but I do have a couple of clients scheduled. The first one is at 12:30 in the afternoon. I was going to do so some studying in the morning for a quiz coming up, but I can look over my papers at the doctor's office. With that client, I just have to verify his information, make some calls, and maybe send out some letters," said Aaron.

Then Aaron rolled over to Anita with a smile and gave her a kiss and a big hug and said, "Our son will soon be a big brother. I'm excited; we can afford another child now. We are making real good money and it's only going to get better. We don't have to hide anything and we are ready for this little one."

The next morning, Aaron and Anita got up. They got Junior up and ready for school. Aaron and Junior ate breakfast, but Anita wanted to wait. She did not know if blood would be drawn. When the time came for the children to go to school, they walked Junior to the car, kissed him, and told all the children to have a good day.

Then they went back into the house for a little more than an hour before Anita's appointment.

The Jacksons went into the examining room and Dr. Cooper came into the room. He said, "Mr. and Mrs. Jackson, why are we here today?"

Anita said, "Dr. Cooper, I've been feeling kind of funny lately, not so much tired, but different. My husband brought it to my attention that, he too, has been feeling different. I have not missed any cycles, but I want to take a pregnancy test, just to see if I am pregnant or not."

Then Dr. Cooper said, "Well, it looks like you have put on a few pounds since your last visit. Your pressure and all your other tests look good. Let me get a urine sample and test it right now."

Dr. Cooper left the examining room for a few minutes. Then Anita went into the bathroom with her specimen cup. When she came out, she put her cup on the table and waited for the doctor to come. When Dr. Cooper came back, he had all that he needed to draw the blood.

Dr. Cooper told Anita, "Ok, I'm going to get a blood sample from you and test it also. It will take about 10 minutes for the results to come back." So he drew the blood and left the office.

While Aaron and Anita waited, Anita said, "If we are pregnant, this would be it. All we need is a brother or sister for Junior."

Aaron said, "You got that right. We have too many plans. If you are pregnant and this child goes to private school that will cost us double, with a small discount, but it will work out."

When Dr. Cooper came back into the room, he said, "Well Jacksons, it looks like you are expecting a baby. I'm going to start you on maternity vitamins and I want you to make an appointment at the desk. I want to see you two back in one month. Even though you have been seeing your cycle, it will stop. So by the time of your next visit, I should be able to measure and see how far you are and give you a delivery day that will range six days before or six days after the date given. Make sure you eat vegetables and fruits, drink water, and don't overeat. Any questions?"

"No sir, we just need to start planning on having another baby in the house," Anita said.

Then Aaron stood, shook the doctor's hand, and said, "Dr. Cooper, we thank you and we will see you in one month."

As they left the office, Aaron said, "I don't know about you, but I'm happy."

Anita said, "So am I, now. Since we are in one car, you have to drop me off at work and pick me up later. I'll call Patsy and let her know, so that she will see that Junior is cared for."

One month had gone by and it was time for Anita's doctor's visit. Aaron went along with her for this visit. They sat in the waiting room to be called.

Aaron said to Anita, "I don't know. Maybe I'm a little too excited about this baby. Do you think that your stomach is bigger than it was when you carried Junior?"

Anita said, "No, it's not. I see that I am bigger this time. Maybe we're having twins. We can really stop then."

When Anita's name was called, they both got up. As they walked down the hall behind the doctor's assistant, Paula, she said, "Dr. Cooper wants to see you in the testing lab first. He wants to see how far along you are. Your husband can come into the room, but he will have to sit behind the curtain, and I will assist the doctor. He will explain everything as he goes."

When they walked into the room, Paula said, "I'll need you to take off everything. You can put on this gown and leave it open in the front. I'll be right back."

Aaron said, "Look at all the equipment that he's using today. We might be having twins. Do you know that's five mouths to feed? I'd better work real hard (and then he let out a giggle)."

Anita changed into her gown and there was a knock on the door. It was Dr. Cooper and Paula.

Dr. Cooper said, "Good morning, Mr. and Mrs. Jackson," then he looked at Anita and said, "How have you been feeling?"

Anita said, "I feel ok, Dr. Cooper. I'm just bigger with this baby!"

"Well, that's the reason why we are in this room today. We are going to test and see how far along you are because your cycle was still coming on. We will measure the size of your cervix and your stomach. So if you will get on the table and put this sheet in front of you, I will start examining you," he said.

Dr. Cooper looked at Anita's stomach and said, "When did you start feeling different?"

Anita said, "About a couple months ago."

As Aaron sat behind the curtain, he said, "Yes, that's around the same time when I started feeling different."

Dr. Cooper completed all of his testing and his assistant left the room.

He told Anita, "Ok, you can get up and get dressed. I'll be back to talk with the both of you."

When Dr. Cooper returned, he said, "I have a lot to talk about and explain. Even though your cycle was still showing up, my measurements show that you are about three months, the sonogram shows. Let me turn the film on so that you both can see. Ok, it shows that you are carrying four babies."

Nita went into her shock mode. With her eyes stretched wide, she looked at Aaron, and his eyes were bucked out of his head.

Then Aaron whistled and said, "Wow! Wo! What? Did you say four babies, Dr. Cooper?"

He turned and looked at the doctor, then he looked at Nita and said, "Did he say four babies?"

Dr. Gary Cooper's response was, "Yes, Mr. Jackson, I did say four babies, and they look like they are all doing fine. Within the next two months, we will be able to tell you the sex of the babies."

Aaron looked back at Anita and said, "I don't know anyone who has quads. We thought we needed our families help with having one child; we're really going to need them now in a big way." He rubbed his head and said, "We'll get through this. Yes, we will. I know one thing; I better start working out. I got to be fit for these four babies.

"We're really going to need to move now, with five children living in two bedrooms. Oh, that will not work. Even though the basement has a den, it will work only for a few months."

Anita hadn't said a word, with her eyes still stretched and mouth wide open.

Dr. Cooper looked at Anita and said, "Mrs. Jackson, I'm looking at you with the same expression on your face ever since I gave you the good news. Are you ok?"

Anita said, "Yes, Dr. Cooper, I am. But I just can't believe you said four babies are growing inside me right now. When I carried Junior, my stomach was really big. I just can't imagine me being able to get larger than that. Where is the room going to come from?"

"Well, Mrs. Jackson, as they grow, you will grow. If it gets to the point where you are uncomfortable, I'll start you on bed rest. But before it gets to that stage, make sure you exercise, walk, continue to drink plenty of water, and keep eating your fruits and vegetables. I am going to make a nutrition plan that you will have to follow. This will help you maintain a healthy blood sugar level and keep your blood pressure under control. I will have it ready tomorrow, you can pick it up at the receptionist's desk. If you don't have any more questions, I will see you in one month. You must maintain a healthy weight. We don't want to start you on any medication!"

"Doc, she is my wife and my friend. I will see that she follows the eating plan and I will stop by tomorrow to pick it up myself," Aaron said.

"Dr. Cooper, I am still in shock. We will see you in one month. I don't want to be on any other medication, so I will follow your nutrition plan. Thank you, Doctor," Anita said.

The next month when the Jacksons came for the prenatal visit, Dr. Cooper said, "Hum, by looking at the chart, it looks like somebody has not been following the plan. The weight you've gained from the day you gave blood work and found out that you were expecting, you weighed 135 lbs. Last month, you weighed 143 lbs., and now you weigh

170 lbs. You put on an extra 27 pounds. Why? What are you eating?"

"Well, Dr. Cooper, I thought carrying four babies, I should eat a little extra, so I did," Anita said.

"No, you don't have to eat a little extra, if you follow the plan. You and the babies will get enough to eat. If you come in next month with a weight gain of over 10 pounds, I'm going to have to put you in the hospital and feed you through an IV," Dr. Cooper said.

"Well, Dr. Cooper, I don't want an IV feeding me, so next month, you will see that I have followed the plan," Anita said.

"Ok," Dr. Cooper said.

As the month went by, Anita did follow the plan. She maintained the weight the doctor was looking for. She, Aaron, and Junior went on daily walks. The walks usually would tire Junior out. So when they returned home, he was ready for a bath, a book, and then bedtime.

Planning could not have been better. The babies were due around Junior's birthday. Again both families would come together for Thanksgiving.

Neither Anita nor Aaron had taken time off from their jobs, all of their leave and vacation time were being saved for when the babies come. The time spent for each doctor's visit was made either before work, after work, or on the weekends. They began planning on how many of everything they would need to buy the four children.

Their family down south knew what was going. They talked daily, and Uncle Bubba, with his camera, was ready to come up and snap some pictures. This was something unreal to all of them, and they couldn't wait.

The next doctor's visit went well. Dr. Cooper told Aaron and Anita that they were going to have to take the babies through cesarean. He explained the involvement with the team of doctors and nurses who would be in the operating room. He showed them a film on multiple births. He made sure they understood everything. Dr. Cooper ordered all needed tests to make sure the development of each baby was normal. He also ran tests on Anita as he was getting her prepared for the surgery. Once all of the tests came back, Dr. Cooper planned to give Anita a date for her delivery.

On the next visit, Dr. Cooper told Aaron and Anita that the babies will be born on November 27th, the day after Thanksgiving. He also told her not to get tempted with all of the food around her.

He also said, "I'm sure you will be able to eat lots of leftovers when you get home."

Anita said, "How long will I have to stay in the hospital?"

Dr. Cooper said, "Six to eight days. It depends on the healing of your incision and your health. We have two more months to go. I need to monitor you every two weeks. Now your last month, I will have to see you weekly. And the last two weeks, I will give you the time for the surgery and the time you will have to meet me at the hospital, ok?"

Anita answered, "Ok."

The months zoomed by. Anita was scheduled to check into the hospital at eleven o'clock in the morning. She gave birth to four healthy baby girls. One weighed 6 lbs. and the other three weighed 5 lbs. and some ounces. Aaron went out in the waiting room to let their parents know that Anita and the babies were doing well. He heard them cry out to the Lord giving thanks that all five of them were doing ok.

Henri and Leslie both got on the phone and started making calls.

Once Anita was taken to her room, they all were able to go in and visit with her and the babies.

Aaron told them that he and Anita would be able to take care of the babies themselves. Both moms disagreed, and so they both decided that they were going to stay in D.C. and help them with the children. All Aaron said was, "Thank you, for how long?"

Anita was in her room with the babies when Leslie and Henri walked into the room. They both started talking at the same time, not understanding anything they said. They were nervous and excited.

The babies were now home. Aaron turned the den into a nursery for them. They each were going to sleep in bassinets until their parents figured out how they would arrange the room for four cribs.

While Aaron and Anita laid in bed, they decided to move into the den and put the girls in their bedroom because it was larger.

The girls were now celebrating their 2nd birthday. They were now talking and they were also very busy. Raising five children was a big job. Everything was extra – extra food, getting up extra early, going to bed extra early, and spending extra time with each one of them. Each child wanted extra love and attention. But Aaron Jr. was no problem, as a matter of fact, he was a good helper. He loved playing with his sisters. He would keep them occupied by reading and singing to them. He went as far as teaching them what he was learning in school.

Aaron and Anita really appreciated what Aaron Jr. was doing, but they didn't want him to become overwhelmed.

When the girls became the age to start kindergarten, Aaron and Anita wanted to move back down south so that they would have childcare providers all around them.

Patsy did not want them to leave. She said, "I think both of you should continue to go to school and complete your master's degrees, work, and save as much money as you can. My family and I love having the chance to see the children grow.

"Let them continue to go to school here and when they start junior high school, you may want to leave then. Why don't you two think about it and let me know your thoughts? They are being taught by some of the same teachers Junior had, and you know they are getting a quality education."

While lying in bed that night, Aaron and Anita started putting their heads together on how to be the best parents they could be for all of the children, without becoming stressed out and tired. So they decided to use the advice Patsy gave to stay in D.C. until the girls were thirteen years old. That's when they would start the seventh grade. Aaron and Anita were learning how to deal with each child's personality. They saw the differences, but they wanted to master all that they needed to better each child's growth.

All the adults in the house spent time with the girls. They observed them while trying to learn the characteristics of each one of them. They noticed that Erin was more bossy, selfish, and intimidating. When she told the girls to be quiet, they did as she said. She ran her sisters with her mouth. They were all very busy. Christian and Destiny were giving, loving, and sharing, while Ebony was shy and somewhat quiet. Ebony played with her siblings, but if she was the only child it would be fine with her.

Aaron Jr. also noticed how Erin's temper was, when she would hit her sisters or take something from them. He would say to her, "You just clocked your sisters; you can't do that to your sisters."

Aaron called Anita at work. He said, "Hey babe, I was thinking. We notice how active the girls are and I was doing some research. Now, it's going to cost us. But, who knows? It may help them later in life!"

Anita said, "Ok, what is it?"

Aaron said, "What I thought about are ways to keep all of the girls busy. We should enroll them in gymnastics, karate, and track, just like we did Junior. They will love it."

"All of that, how?" Anita said.

Then Aaron said, "They will go to gymnastics on Tuesdays, run track on Thursdays, and karate on Saturday. Trust me, it will work. We have more than a bundle. If we did it for Junior, we can do it for the girls!"

Anita said, "So, when is this all supposed to start?"

Aaron said, "Next week."

Anita's response was, "Ok, if you feel its best and we can do this. Let's try it."

"Ok, I'll see you at home later. I love you," Aaron said.

"I love you too, see you later," Anita said.

During karate classes, when Erin's time came to compete, Aaron Jr. would say, "Go clock it."

All the girls learned quickly. They earned trophies and only had one more belt to go – their black belt. The girls were really good in all three activities.

They were now in the fifth grade and they stuck together like glue. The sisters were being teased at school by some little white boys. They had to run home lots of times from these bullies.

One day during lunchtime, while in the cafeteria, those boys teased the girls and called them names. Destiny went over to one of the teachers, who was white, and said to her, "Ms. White, those boys are bothering me and my sisters. They are disrespecting us!"

Ms. White said, "Maybe they want to play."

Destiny then said, "They are calling us bad names."

"They will stop. Just ignore them. Go finish your lunch," Ms. White insisted.

Destiny turned and walked back to her seat.

Erin said, "What did she say?"

Destiny said, "Ms. White said they will stop and to ignore them!"

Then Erin said, "I'm not going to keep on ignoring these boys. That's what we have been doing all the time, but have they stopped? No. So what I am going to do is talk with Mom and Dad this evening, while we are eating dinner. And all three of you better tell your part."

So that evening, while having dinner, just like a normal evening, they all talked about their day and if they had any problems with classwork or whatever.

After Aaron blessed the food, Erin said, "Mom and Dad, I have something I want to talk about!"

Then Anita said, "Go right ahead, baby."

Erin said, "There are four white boys who go to our school. They are always messing with us every day in the hallway and in the cafeteria. Don't they? (She looked at her sisters and they nodded their heads in agreement.) Like today, they called us out of our name. Destiny went to tell Ms. White; she is one of the teachers who monitored the cafeteria while we ate lunch. Ms. White told Des to ignore them. This happened before, she said the same thing. They chased us one day. They threw rocks at us. Mom and Dad, you know I will hurt those boys, but I don't want to get in any trouble!"

Aaron said, "How long has this been going on?"

"For a while," Erin said.

"Well, I'm going to pay the school a visit in the morning," Aaron said.

Then Junior said, "Can I come with you, Dad. I want to see who these boys are. Messing with my sisters, which would not happen if I was still going to that school." Then he looked at Erin and said, "Did you clock it, sis?"

"The answer for you Junior is, no, and what can you do?" Erin said.

Junior said, "I will have to tell them not to mess with my sisters. You know I don't play when it comes to my sisters."

Aaron said, "No, I will take care of this."

Then Anita said to Aaron, "Honey, do you think we need to start packing so that we can move down to Florida?"

"No, we are not going to run. We agreed to move to Florida when the girls get out of the sixth grade. They are in the fifth grade, and we are not going anywhere. Until then, I am not going to pay all this money for my children to go to school and have to be harassed or bullied. I don't care whose children they are, or what color they are," Aaron said.

The next morning, Aaron got up and got dressed. They ate breakfast.

Aaron said, "Girls, go grab your books and whatever else you need. Come on, let's go, I'm taking you to school this morning!"

Aaron told Junior, "You have a good day, son."

Junior said, "You too, Dad." And then he winked his eye at Erin and said, "You better clock it. I mean that situation!"

Aaron gave Anita a kiss and told her, "I will call you once I get to the office."

So the girls went into their room, got their things, and out the door they went.

While driving, Ebony sat up front. Aaron told Ebony to look into the glove box and get his tape recorder out. She reached into the glove box and got the recorder. He told her to press the record button, and she did.

Then Ebony said, "What are you recording, Daddy?"

Aaron said, "Press the stop button, then press rewind and play!"

Ebony did as she was told. When she pressed the play button, they could hear what Ebony just said.

"Why did you record us talking, Daddy?" Ebony then said.

"I was just making sure that the batteries are strong. I may have to record the conversation at the school," Aaron said.

When the Jacksons pulled onto the parking lot, Christian said with a very strong voice and pointing, "Daddy, there's one of the boys. He's the one carrying the red and black backpack!"

"Ok, he'll be in the office real soon!" Aaron replied.

Aaron turned the car off and they all got out. While walking towards the school, Aaron and the girls heard a voice that said, "Black beaver."

Ebony's teeth protruded some and she was going to get braces soon. When they heard the voice, she said, "Daddy, he's the one with the Mohawk haircut!"

Aaron said, "How do you know?"

"I know because he has called me that many times," she said.

"Just keep walking. Right now, we are going to ignore the stupidity!" Aaron said.

As they approached the school, the principal was standing outside greeting the students. His name was Mr. Stonewall.

"Good morning, Mr. Jackson, Ebony, Erin, Destiny, and Christian," he said.

They all said, "Good morning."

Then Aaron said, "Mr. Stonewall, I'll be waiting in the office when you are done with your morning routine."

Mr. Stonewall said, "Ok sir, I'll see you shortly."

The Jacksons went into the building. Aaron kissed each child on the forehead. Then he said, "Go on to class. If I need any of you, I'll have the office to contact your class. Have a good day."

The girls walked down the hall and Aaron went into the office. He walked up to the desk and told the lady that he was waiting for Mr. Stonewall, then he took a seat.

The bell rang. It was the start of the day for the students. A few minutes later, Mr. Stonewall walked into the office. Aaron stood up and Mr. Stonewall said, "Mr. Jackson, you may come into my office."

As Aaron walked into the office, Mr. Stonewall stood at the door and closed the door behind them. He walked over and sat behind his desk.

Mr. Stonewall said, "What brings you here today, Mr. Jackson?"

Mr. Jackson said, "Well, Mr. Stonewall, last night, while having dinner with my family, my daughter Erin was very disturbed. It's gotten to the point that they are tired of running. My girls are being harassed and bullied and I will not have that."

Mr. Stonewall said, "Oh no, I agree; we won't tolerate that kind of behavior in this school."

"Well, according to my girls, it has been going on for a while and they are no longer going to put up with it. I'm just finding out about this and it has to stop today," Mr. Jackson said.

"Who, may I ask is harassing your daughters?" Mr. Stonewall asked.

"Well, Mr. Stonewall, I don't know the names of the four boys," Aaron said, as he looked at him.

So Mr. Stonewall called Erin to his office to get their names. Once she left his office, Aaron said, "Ok, Mr. Stonewall, how are we going to handle this?"

"Well, Mr. Jackson, I think I'm going to speak with each one of those boys and see what's been going on," he said.

"And when do you plan on doing that, sir?" Aaron asked.

"Well, I don't know if today is a good day. I would have to call each one of them out of their class," Mr. Stonewall said.

"Well, I do know that today is a good day. It's a day that the Lord has made. You called my child out of her class, Mr. Stonewall. I know you know that I've given this school a lot of money, and one thing I don't do is throw my money away. Unless you want me to go to the School Board when I leave here, I think you need to have someone call each one of those boys out of their class," Mr. Jackson said.

Mr. Stonewall got out of his chair and said, "Give me a minute." He walked over to the door and told Sally, "The names I'm giving you (he called out each name), I need you to call these boys down to the office."

He also told her to, "Wait until one comes down, then call the next one, and make sure that they don't sit next to each other while waiting to come into my office!"

"Yes sir," Sally said.

Sally called the boys down to the office. Three of them came quickly and were sitting as they waited for the fourth one to come down.

"I know these boys. They come from a prominent background. Their parents are really big in the government. How will I approach them about this?" Mr. Stonewall said.

Then Mr. Jackson said, "Mr. Stonewall, my children come from a very prominent background as well, but they know how to respect others and themselves. If someone comes to me and tells me that my child has been acting out of character, believe me, Mr. Stonewall, the next time that person sees my child, they will know that their dad handled that situation. You got to know how to deal with your children. Now as far as you approaching these boys' parents, just tell them the allegations that have been brought against them, explain what was said, and that's all you need to do!

"If you can't do it, then I will. Oh, by the way, Ms. White is the teacher my child went to more than once while in the cafeteria to tell her that those boys were harassing them, and she told my girls to ignore them. I think we need to talk to her also. Now I have not sat with each one of my girls to find out all that has been going on, and I pray that this is it. Let me remind you, I am one of the highest paid attorneys in the district's courthouse, and I got that way because I never lose a case. I don't lie. I just tell it like it is. Oh, I will be recording each one of those boys and Ms. White."

Now that the fourth boy was in the office, Mr. Stonewall called them in his office, one at a time. He called Peter in first. He introduced Peter to Mr. Jackson and told him who Mr. Jackson was.

"Peter, have you been harassing the Jackson girls and calling them out of their name," Mr. Stonewall said.

"No sir," Peter said.

"You are the boy wearing the Mohawk. You called my child a black beaver this morning. Mr. Stonewall, I think a letter needs to go out to his parents and you need to make a call to this child's parents. I'm not going to stand for these lies. I recognize voices, and your voice is what I heard this morning," Mr. Jackson said.

"Well Peter, I'm going to have to suspend you, because what you said was unacceptable, and you did it in front of an adult. He is the girls' father. You will be out for the rest of this week until next Tuesday. That will be a five-day suspension. You may complete the rest of this day," Mr. Stonewall said.

Then he called Richard in. Mr. Stonewall introduced Mr. Jackson. Then he said, "Richard, it has been brought to my attention that you have been harassing the Jackson girls. Have you?"

"Well, sometimes, I'm not going to lie. Yes, we have been. Those girls are A students. They think they are better than everyone else. I don't hit girls, but if I could, I would. I was going to make my sister kick their butts. That's why we threw rocks at them. Y'all called me in here for this; me and my boys don't like them," Richard said, as he slouched down in the chair with his hand between his legs.

Mr. Jackson looked Richard in his eyes and said, "Let me say something to you, boy. My girls are A students because they study and they study hard. If you are jealous of them, that's a problem you have within yourself. You said that if you could hit my girls you would. I don't promote fighting, but I'd like to see you try it. Just put your hand on either one of them, and see what you'll get. If you love your sister, I advise you not to ask her to approach any of my children. And if you throw another rock at them, you will be in court with assault charges. And the next time you see them, you better just keep walking right past them. You are too young to have the attitude that you have. Ask your parents to get you some help. You need help!"

"I don't need help-" Richard said.

Mr. Stonewall cut him off. "Son, I am shocked at your behavior. I will have to suspend you for three weeks. Your parents will be notified and they must return back to school with you. You will complete this day out. You can leave my office now."

Mr. Stonewall called Bobby in his office. As he walked in, he said, "Y'all must be cutting throats in here today. My boys are pissed at y'all."

Mr. Stonewall said, "Sit down, Bobby. I am getting fed up with the nonsense. Your boys have been put out of school today. Now, I called you down here because you and your boys have been harassing the Jackson girls. Why?"

"For real, Mr. Stonewall. My family don't like blacks. My parents may pretend like they do, but we don't!" Bobby said.

"And may I ask why?" Mr. Jackson said.

"Because we don't. We don't have to have a reason why," Bobby said.

"Well, young man, let me say first that each one of you boys are being recorded. Regardless of someone's color, my girls are black. Their parents are black. Their grandparents and great-grandparents are black, and we are proud of it. You need to read up on black history and learn a little something. Because of who my ancestors were, makes me who I am today – a strong black man, who's not going to take any mess from anyone that has a problem with my color. No judge is going to like hearing that you or your parents don't like black people just because we are not white. Don't harass my girls. When you see them, I advise you to look the other way," Mr. Jackson said.

"Bobby, I didn't like what I heard coming from your mouth today. I am a white man and you are a white boy, and right now, I don't like you. You will be on suspension until further notice. I will send a letter to your parents and to the guidance counselor, requiring therapy. You will finish out today. You may leave my office," Mr. Stonewall said.

As Bobby walked out of the office, he said to Billy, "Man, those black girls got me suspended."

Mr. Jackson stood up, but Mr. Stonewall said, "Please sir, I know how you feel. They will be dealt with."

"Billy," Mr. Stonewall called his name. Billy came into his office and said, "I know what this is about. I ain't did nothing."

"Sit down, Billy; we already know what you have done to the Jackson girls. Now, I'm telling you that it has to stop today. Why are you following those boys?" Mr. Stonewall said.

"They are my friends," Billy said.

"If your friends do something or tell you to do something that you know is wrong, are you going to do it?" Mr. Stonewall said.

"Maybe, maybe not," Billy said.

"Well Billy, do you know if you hang with the wrong crowd and they do something that is not right, do you know that you will be charged the same as them? That maybe, maybe not attitude will not get you far," Mr. Stonewall said.

"Mr. Stonewall did not tell you that I don't play when it comes to my children. If they don't bother you, please don't bother them. I don't want to see you in court and I don't want to come back up to the school with more problems coming from you and your boys. Think with your own head," Mr. Jackson said.

"Billy, I'm going to have to suspend you for one week, starting tomorrow. You will finish today out. And son, while you are out, I hope that you find better friends. I'll be sending a letter home to your parents. You may now go back to class," Mr. Stonewall said.

Billy walked out the door. Mr. Stonewall said, "Close the door behind you."

Mr. Stonewall got up and walked to the door. He said, "Sally, I'm going to need you. Oh, never mind."

"Ms. White, can you come down to my office?" he said, over the intercom.

Ms. White walked into the office. She saw Mr. Jackson. He stood, and then Mr. Stonewall said, "Ms. White, this is Mr. Jackson, he's the father of the Jackson girls."

They shook hands. Ms. White said, "Please to meet you, Mr. Jackson."

Mr. Jackson said, "I'm happy to meet you."

Mr. Stonewall said, "Please sit."

Then Mr. Stonewall said, "Ms. White, I called you into my office because the Jackson girls came to you several times on different occasions, letting you know that they were being harassed, and you ignored them. Harassment and bullying are not tolerated in this school. Can you tell me your side?"

"Well, Mr. Stonewall, Mr. Jackson, the girls have come to me, but I didn't think it was that serious," she said.

"Well, what is serious to you, Ms. White?" Mr. Stonewall said.

"An argument or if a fight breaks out, that's serious," Ms. White said.

"Ms. White, being harassed is serious; this has been going on for a while now. You should have brought this to my attention. This is unacceptable and I hold you responsible for not handling the situation in a better fashion. I'm sorry, Ms. White, but I'm going to have to bring in a substitute for your class for two days, while you are out on suspension. This will start tomorrow. I have to call the School Board about this!" said Mr. Stonewall.

"Ms. White, my girls are not just any children. They are young innocent girls. They are smart, respectable, and they are mine. I love my children. Please don't ignore them or any other child when they come to you; it could be a matter of life or death," Mr. Jackson said.

"Well, I do want to apologize. I'm sorry," Ms. White said.

"Apology is accepted. I don't know if you are a mother or not, just put yourself in a parent's shoes when you deal with children," Mr. Jackson said.

"Ms. White, you may continue with what you were doing before you were called to the office, thank you," Mr. Stonewall said.

After Ms. White left the office, Mr. Jackson stood up and extended his hand. As they shook hands, he said, "Mr. Stonewall, I thank you. I didn't know how this was going to turn out. Now I can report back to my wife, who I know is on pins and needles waiting to hear from me, and also my son."

"How is Aaron Jr. doing?" Mr. Stonewall asked.

"He's doing really well. He was accepted into the Air Force Academy. He will be leaving home soon. He has his mind focused on his future. Sir, I hope that this is the end of this and there will be no retaliations behind any of this. Just think, this is elementary school. Can you imagine if this group of boys were in high school? It would be a total mess!" Mr. Jackson said.

As Mr. Jackson left the office, he said to the ladies working in the office, "Good day, ladies," and walked out the door.

When Mr. Jackson got to work, he called his wife. She answered the phone and said, "What happened?"

Aaron said, "Well, I hope everything is taken care of. Those four little hellions have been suspended, along with Ms. White. I let Mr. Stonewall know that I didn't come up here to play and I was not leaving until this matter was taken care of."

There was peace in the school for a short time, but those four monkeys did not learn. The girls were now in the sixth grade and will soon graduate and move to Florida. They told their dad that the boys continued to mess with them.

One day, just before graduation, the girls were walking home from school. It was a nice day. They ran into none other than the four monkeys. As they continued to walk, the girls started talking to each other. They said, "We are not going to run and if those guys put their hands on us, they are going to get a serious butt kicking."

So, they got up to where the boys were and they kept walking. Bobby and Richard put their hands on two of the sisters. The girls went into their karate stance and their minds zoned out. They whipped those boys' tails. They did not get off of them until the boys started yelling for help. They broke a leg, a wrist, and an arm. The other one will need plenty of makeup because he received a lot of hard knocks in the face.

When the girls got home, their parents were already there. They saw how their clothes were torn and nervously asked what happened.

"Come sit down," their parents said.

Aaron said, "I need one of you to tell your mom and me what happened!"

Destiny said, "Well, Mom and Dad, we were walking home and ran into the same four boys. As we were approaching them, we started talking to each other and saying, 'We are not going to run from these guys, we are going to keep walking, but if they put their hands on us, we will kick their butts,' and that's what we did."

"Well, I'm not going to say good for you girls, but I will say that I am happy you all are ok, and that you stood up to them," Aaron said.

"Did you get them good?" Anita asked.

"Mama, we beat those boys so bad, we gave them something they will never forget. You'll see them at graduation. I'm so glad we don't have to be around them anymore; we clocked them," Erin said.

On graduation day, the four boys showed up looking jacked up. Those sisters put a hurting on them and they were too ashamed to say that girls beat their tails. They walked across the stage wearing casts and bruised faces.

Aaron Jr.'s last two years of high school were at the Air Force Academy in Colorado. They saw his potential and the officers were very impressed with him, which prompted the Academy to enroll him into the acceleration programs. Junior was able to be home for his sisters' graduation and was tickled when he saw those boys. He said to himself,

"I know my sisters clocked all four of you real good."

Aaron and Anita agreed to stay at Patsy's house until the girls graduated from the sixth grade. They were now preparing themselves to move, so they were taking care of all their necessary business.

Meanwhile, the girls were in the bedroom talking and they were not happy about the move to Florida. They wanted to live in South Carolina for a while.

Aaron and Anita could hear them talking. Aaron said, "I wouldn't mind moving back home. What do you think about that?"

Then Anita said, "I understand how they feel. We need more space and I do miss being around our family!"

Both Aaron and Anita were homesick, and they knew that they couldn't live with Patsy and her family forever, but they were not ready to move to Florida.

Money was not an issue for them. Their finances were really good, but they didn't want to live that far of a distance away from everyone. They were now thinking hard about moving back to South Carolina to be with family, friends, and let the girls become active members of Mount Anna.

Their minds were now made up; they decided to let the girls go to school in South Carolina until they graduated from high school.

Aaron and Anita did not want to go back home without having their own home, so the family packed up and drove to South Carolina every other Friday. They spent an entire weekend looking for a house they would love. They wanted something big enough for all of them and any guest that would come to visit.

When Anita and Aaron first started looking for a house, they arrived in South Carolina and went to their parents' homes. They did not tell them why they were in town, but Leslie and Henri thought that they were only coming for a short visit. The girls stayed with the grandparents, while Aaron and Anita went out looking at homes. But before they left, Henri said, "Why don't we go out for dinner tonight?"

Aaron said, "That's sounds good. We will meet with y'all a little later," and then they walked out the door.

Later that evening, while having dinner, Aaron's and Anita's parents gave them the keys to the Florida home. They were lost for words. At the time, they did not know how to tell their parents that they were not ready to move to Florida.

So Aaron asked the parents, "How did y'all buy that house?"

Aaron's dad, Lamont, said, "We may have not had everything we wanted to give to our children, but you never went hungry. We always kept a roof over your heads and we saved our money every chance we could. Never forget, our Father is rich in houses and land."

Then Aaron said, "Well, I don't know how to say this, but –"

After Aaron paused, Henri said, "Not another baby, don't tell us that."

"Five children, we are done having babies. We have enough, but that's not what we want to say," Anita said.

Anita looked at Aaron and said, "Go on Ron, tell them."

Aaron said, "Right now, at this time, we are not ready to move to Florida. Nita and I feel that we will be too far from our family. We thank you wholeheartedly."

Then Henri said, "Well, what are y'all going to do? You said when the girls went to the seventh grade, you would move into the house. The girls are getting older. Y'all can't live in Patsy's basement forever, so what you gonna do?"

Anita said, "We're working on some things. As soon as we iron them out, we will let y'all know."

"Ok," Henri said, "we hope you are making wise decisions."

"We are doing what's best for our children and us, you'll see," Anita said.

Aaron's and Anita's sisters and brothers were now grown adults with college degrees and working. Some were living on their own, but they were still close. They talked on the phone almost every day. During the holidays, the families still came together.

One day, Lindsey, who is the oldest of Aaron's sisters, was working at one of the plants. While at work, an explosion occurred. The loud blast caused her to lose hearing in both ears. In order for the family to communicate, she and the entire family learned sign language.

Aaron and Anita looked at many homes. Some were either too small, not enough yard space, or the location wasn't suitable enough for them; so they kept looking. The day before they were going back to D.C. was when they saw a house that they both loved. It was fenced in. The house had a long circular driveway and the landscaping was beautiful. It had six bedrooms, a three-car garage, and it was in a nice neighborhood and in a good location.

When Aaron and Anita saw that house, they contacted their realtor and asked if they could get the code to see inside of the house. They did their own walkthrough. They flushed the toilets. They turned on all the lights and looked for water damage. They ran the dishwasher. Aaron took his shirt off and ran water on it. He put it in the dryer to make sure it worked. They turned on the washing machine and let it run its course. They turned on the air conditioner, then the heater, and the hot water. They looked at the furnace to see when it was put in. They checked the carpet and flooring underneath. They raised the windows to make sure that they stayed up and even checked the weather stripping around the doors.

After they did their thorough check, they walked around the outside, and then they called their real estate agent. They told her they wanted that house and they were on the way to her office to fill out the papers.

So they met with the agent and filled out all the papers. They wrote a check for the deposit. They made sure that they had someone to oversee all the inspections and they got a tentative closing date.

While driving back to D.C., Anita told the children about their plans of moving back to South Carolina until they went to college. She asked the girls not to tell their grandparents about what's going to take place, because they wanted to surprise them.

Even though Aaron's and Anita's parents were looking forward to them moving into their home in Florida, they knew that they would be happier knowing that they decided to move closer to family for a while. The girls were very excited knowing that they would be living around their relatives and maybe attend the same school their parents attended. They planned to move to Florida when the girls attend college. They felt that the school in Florida would be best for what the girls wanted to major in and it would be a good start for their future.

Once they returned home, Aaron and Anita sat down with Chris and Patsy. They told them what their plans were and about the new home that they put a contract on. Patsy was happy for them. She and Chris were both glad that they were not moving to Florida right away.

When the girls started the seventh grade, Aaron and Anita wanted them to study a foreign language. They sat and discussed it with the girls and explained how it would benefit them later. They wanted each child to study a different language. That way they can teach each other a different language; so they decided on French, Spanish, Chinese, and Latin.

Aaron and Anita let the girls decide on the language they would study. They knew that the girls would not think twice about it because their brother already knew how to speak all four languages fluently.

The Jacksons did get the home. Very early one morning, they began packing up ready to move. They loaded up the moving truck that they rented.

It was a tear-jerking time as everyone helped. Chris and Patsy talked about how Aaron and Anita were young adults eager to learn and grow. They talked about how they watched the children grow up thriving in the basement, while one was off in the Air Force Academy. They reminisced about the fun and funny times they shared with the four, now teenagers.

Aaron called everyone he knew in town that could help them unload the truck when they arrived at their new home. He also let them know that they were surprising their parents and not to say a word.

They got on the road for the eight-hour drive. Anita drove their truck, while Aaron drove the rental with a trailer pulling their car. The eight-hour trip turned out to be seven hours. The excitement caused their feet to hit the accelerator just a little harder.

When they pulled up into the driveway of their home, on a Friday night, all of the heavy hitters came out of the house. Anita's brother had a key. When Aaron and his family got out of the truck, they hugged everyone. The helpers talked about how nice the house was and then they started to unload the truck. They worked until everything was out of the vehicles.

On Saturday, Anita and the girls got up and started unpacking, while Aaron and his brother went to return the truck and buy some food.

Aaron and his brother saw their dad while they were downtown and they had to hide. When they saw they were in the clear, they went into the grocery store.

On Monday morning, Anita and Aaron were off for a week before they started working at their new jobs. They needed time to take care of business for themselves and things for the girls. The girls were out of school for their summer break, and Anita wanted to make sure that they stayed busy. She enrolled them back into gymnastics and a dance class. She also had two days set aside for them to spend time in the library.

Aaron and Anita thought about how they could get their parents over to their new home without letting them know that they have moved back home.

While they talked with their mothers on the phone, Anita told them that they would be in town on Friday and they were all invited to have dinner at the Blackmon's in their new home. She also told them not to mention it to the Blackmons because it was going to be a surprise birthday dinner for Mrs. Blackmon, so they both agreed not to say a word, not even to their husbands.

Anita told their moms that they would arrive at the Blackmon's around 6:30 in the evening because Mrs. Blackmon will be away from the house. She also said that Mr. Blackmon asked if she and Aaron would tell their parents to meet them around that same time and also tell our siblings to come join them. Both moms said, "Ok."

Anita then called Bubba. He answered the phone and said, "Hey girl, where are you? You in town?"

Then Anita asked, "Uncle Bubba, what are you doing on Friday around 5:30?"

Anita said, "Yes, I am. My family and I bought a house here and we are going to be staying in Aiken until the girls graduate from high school, then we're moving to Florida while they attend college."

Uncle Bubba said, "Nobody told me that y'all moved back!"

"That's because nobody knows, except our sisters and brothers. We want to surprise our parents. That's why I'm calling you. We are going to have dinner at our house on Friday and we want you to be here before they arrive. When I open the door, I want you to be standing inside to get snapshots of the shocking look on their faces," Anita said.

Uncle Bubba said, "Oh yeah, I will be there. Oh boy, I can see their jaws drop now. So what street y'all moved on?"

"Cherokee Street," Anita said.

Uncle Bubba said, "Cherokee Street, that big pretty house that was for sale. Y'all bought that one?"

"Yes, we did," Anita said.

"Aw shucks, I'll be there at 5:00. I'm excited now. I'll see you on Friday. Talk with you later," Uncle Bubba said.

"Ok, see you then," Anita said.

When Friday evening came, everyone but Anita met in front of what they thought was the Blackmon's driveway.

Henri asked Ebony, "Where is your mama?"

Ebony said, "She's in the house."

"Well, I guess she's helping the family get things together for the surprise. Let's go on in, they may need us to help out too," Henri said.

So they drove up in the driveway and Leslie said, "This sure is a beautiful house. Then they parked their cars and walked up to the door. They rung the bell and Anita answered the door and said, "Surprise, welcome to our home!"

Leslie said with a high-pitched voice, "Our home!"

"Whose home?" Henri said.

As Nita stood laughing at the look on their faces, while Bubba snapped pictures, she said, "Come on in, this is our new home."

"Well, well, well, Les, they really pulled a fast one on us," Henri said.

"Yes, they did," Leslie said.

"How long have y'all been living in this house? From the looks of things, you had to have been here for a month," Henri said.

As they walked around from room to room, Leslie said, "We don't see any bags or boxes."

"We moved in last Friday," Aaron said.

"Last Friday, last Friday! We were talking to y'all every day on the phone thinking that you're still at Patsy's, and you were down here. This is a beautiful home. We really got fooled this time. I see you've been busy. Nobody told us a thing," said Leslie.

Mr. and Mrs. Blackmon, along with other friends and family, were at the house welcoming dinner.

Leslie brought a big plant; Henri brought a huge hanging mirror, thinking that the gift was for the Blackmons. They also received other nice gifts.

After dinner was over, they all pitched in to help clean, then everyone went home and the Jacksons went to bed.

Both Aaron and Anita loved a beautiful yard. They got up the next morning and did yard work, planting flowers and trees.

On Sunday, they all went to church and had a wonderful time. The girls joined Mount Anna and they were active in the church.

Aaron and Anita were back to work. The girls were back in school. They talked about how happy they were to be away from those four bullies. The girls were pleased with their activities after school. Anita made sure that all of the classes the girls were taking would benefit them in high school and college.

Aaron Jr. came home for a month. While he was home, he spent lots of time with his sisters, teaching them the different languages that he speaks. He also talked with them about his jobs in the Air Force in Law Enforcement and Forensic Science; he loved both jobs. When he leaves, his next assignment will be in Germany for a few years. But before he left, he told Erin, "Do your best. Clock those grades. Knock them out. And if anyone bothers you, I know you better clock them."

Then Christian said, "Junior, you have been telling Erin to clock it ever since we were little. Exactly what does clock it mean?"

"Well Chris, clock it is not a bad thing. Instead of saying go knock them out or knock it out, whether it's work, play, kicking butt, or whatever you're focused on, do your best and go for it. But when you say clock it, you got to wink your eye and click your teeth, just like this," Junior said.

While stationed in Germany, Junior kept in touch with his family and talked with them almost daily. He loved his sisters and he was proud of the young ladies they had become. He was also happy about the choices they chose for their own paths of study in college.

COLLEGE CRIMINALS

Chapter Six

Now that Christian, Erin, Destiny, and Ebony were all in college, they thought the nightmare of being bullied was gone, and yet it still existed.

Their first year of school was good. The girls studied very hard. They stayed in the school library and they kept their focus on their degrees by keeping their honor roll status and staying on the Dean's list.

Erin was majoring in Sports Medicine. Ebony wanted to be in Broadcasting. Christian was studying Mortuary Science, and Destiny was studying to become a Journalist.

Erin said, "Chris, when I walked out of the bathroom at school today, I was going down the hall. I looked up and I thought I saw Peter Pitts!"

"Who is Peter Pitts?" With a shocked look on her face, Christian said, "Not the boy from elementary school!"

"Yes, him," Erin said.

"No way, it couldn't be," Christian said.

"He looked a lot older, but I really think it was him. I only had a glimpse of his face and that Mohawk. After that, I got an eerie feeling," Erin said.

Then Destiny told Ebony, "I think I saw Bobby Spinks today in the bookstore on campus. He looked at me and gave me the middle finger. My heart dropped; I was frozen stiff."

"Are you sure it was him?" Ebony said.

"Yes, I'm sure. I know what those ugly boys look like, young or old," Destiny said.

"Well, I'll tell you what, we don't work out daily for nothing and we don't break two-by-fours in half with our hands for nothing. We don't run three miles a day for nothing, and if they cross us wrongly, we will show them that our parents' money did not go to waste. We are not going to live in fear and that's all I am going to say about that," Erin said.

"Should we tell Dad?" Destiny said.

"Yes, we should. We need to make Christian and Ebony aware also," Erin said.

Because these young ladies were talented, pretty, and smart, they were really hated by four white boys and envied by some of the girls who were attending the school.

While walking to their car after class, someone blew a dart and it hit Ebony on the leg. First, they panicked. Then the sisters got into the car and drove Ebony to the hospital.

The police were called and a report was filed. Ebony got a tetanus shot. The doctor wrapped her leg and they went home.

Their parents were at home when the girls arrived. They saw Ebony's leg wrapped up and their dad asked, "What happened?"

Ebony said, "Someone blew a dart and it struck me on the leg."

"A dart? What is going on? Who would do something like that? Did you girls call the police?" Aaron asked.

Ebony said, "Yes, the hospital did and they filed a report."

"Let me see that report," Aaron said.

Ebony gave the police report to her dad. He read it and said, "This officer right here is racist. I'm going to make sure he turned this report over to the right hands."

Then Destiny said, "Dad, I think it was one of the boys who harassed us when we were in elementary school. I told Ebony today that I saw Bobby Spinks."

"Ah, I saw Peter Pitts," Erin said.

"Wait a minute, what did the both of you just say? Are you talking about those boys I had to come up to your elementary school about? Are they attending the same school?" Aaron asked, with a serious look of concern on his face.

"Ok, I have to deal with this quickly. This can't be happening. How ironic is this? I'll tell you what, no, I can't say what I'm thinking. But what I will say is that I will protect my family any way necessary, you can believe that. I'm calling up to the school right now," Aaron said.

Aaron got on the phone and called up to the school. Lauren Wright answered the call, "Hi, this is Lauren, how may I help you?"

"Lauren, hi, this is Aaron Jackson. My daughters are the Jackson quads attending school there!"

"Oh yes, Mr. Jackson, how can I help you?" Lauren asked.

"Well Lauren, today after school, my daughter Ebony was struck on the leg with a blow dart. A police report was filed at the hospital. She's ok, but it could have been very serious!" Mr. Jackson said.

"Oh no, not here at the school?" Lauren said.

"Oh yes, right there at the school, in the parking lot. Lauren, I have four names and I need you to tell me if any of them are attending the school." Aaron said.

"Ok sir, what are the names?" Lauren said.

"Peter Pitts, Richard Rivers, Billy Goldstein, and Bobby Spinks," Aaron said.

"Hold one second while I look those names up, please," Lauren said.

Then Lauren came back on the phone and said, "I'm sorry, Mr. Jackson, none of the four names are enrolled in our school!"

"I thank you for checking," Aaron said, and the call ended.

The next day, while at school, Erin was walking down the hall and someone came up from behind and hit her on the back of the head with a hard object. It knocked her out and she fell to the floor. Her head was bleeding, but there was no one around. She tried to get up, but she was too dizzy to move.

Around the same time as Erin laid on the floor bleeding, Christian was slashed with a razor on the back of her neck. She immediately went into shock, as she touched the cut and saw blood. She applied pressure to her neck, as she walked in a daze for help.

Someone was walking down the hall; they screamed when they saw Erin lying on the floor and they ran for help.

Alarms rang out on campus. They locked all doors and this alerted Destiny and Ebony. They panicked while looking for their sisters. They ran up the stairs and down the halls. Someone told them that the ambulance was outside, taking their sisters to the hospital. So they ran, and as soon as they reached the outside, the ambulance was driving off.

Ebony and Destiny ran to their car only to find that all four tires were slashed. Their first thought was to run over to the first officer that they saw who was a white police officer.

Then Ebony said, "No, let's go to the black officer." So they ran over to one of the black police officers that was on the scene and explained to him that the two girls in the ambulance were their sisters and that someone slashed their car tires.

With tears in her eyes, Ebony said, "Officer, will you please take us to the hospital?"

"Sure, I will. There is my cruiser. Come on, girls."

The officer drove with the siren on to the hospital. Ebony said, "Officer, we thank you. What is your name, sir?"

"Officer Jeffery Harrison," he said, as he passed Ebony his business card.

Ebony took the card and said, "Thank you."

Then Destiny said, "Officer, what happened?"

"Well, young lady, I really don't want to worry you, but I will say that both your sisters were injured and it is under investigation," Officer Harrison said.

As they pulled up at the hospital and the officer stopped the car, he said, "I hope your sisters will be ok. If I can be of any help, you have my card, just call my number."

Both girls said, "Thank you," and they ran towards the hospital's doors.

Ebony and Destiny ran into the hospital and up to the desk. Their dad saw them and called out their names. They ran over to him and he hugged both of them. He consoled them as they cried. "It's going to be ok," he said.

They took a seat. Then Ebony said, "What happened, Daddy?"

Aaron said, "Well, it looks like Erin was hit in the back of the head with a hard object, like a pipe. It knocked her out and someone saw her lying in the hall bleeding, and they ran for help. Your mom came out just seconds before you came in the door, looking for both of you. I called the school and I was informed that a police officer was bringing both of you here because someone slashed the tires on your car. Chris was cut on the back of her neck. The doctors said a few more inches it would have hit her spinal cord. I think they are both going to be ok, but they will have to spend the night in the hospital, just to be observed. Your mom will talk with us when she comes out here."

"Here, Daddy," Ebony said, as she handed the police officer's card.

She said, "This card is the police officer who drove us here and he said if he can help in any way, just call him."

"Thanks, baby. I will be calling him. Did anyone see who slashed the tires on the car?" Aaron said.

"We're not sure. A student in the hallway saw Ebony and me running. We were looking for Christian and Erin, right when the alarm sounded and the announcement was made that the school was on lockdown. That's when she said to us, 'Your sisters are on the way to the hospital,'" Destiny said.

"Well, who was the girl? You keep saying she," Aaron said.

"I don't know her name, but I do know that she is a student and she takes a class with Erin," Destiny answered.

"Let me call Officer Harrison right now and find out what's going on at the school. I need to see if he will assist the tow truck driver. I'll be right back," Aaron said.

Aaron walked outside and took the officer's business card out of his pocket. He looked at it and started dialing the number. While he was dialing, he said, "First thing in the morning, I'm getting my entire family one of these cellular phones."

The officer answered and said, "This is Officer Harrison!"

Aaron said, "Officer Harrison, hi, my name is Attorney Aaron Jackson. I'm the father of the girls you dropped off at the hospital. I really thank you for taking the time to do that. Can you tell me what happened, and has anyone been arrested for what they did to my daughters?"

Meanwhile, back in the treatment area of the hospital, Anita was running back and forth from room to room, checking on her girls.

She was boiling over with so many emotions running through her right then. She said to herself, "I wish I could find who did this and just ring their necks. I am to the point, if anyone comes to me with some dumb stuff, I don't think my professionalism will be seen. These are my babies, and I know that child of mine (she was thinking about Erin). When she heals, ooh boy, watch out. She's going to go for blood. I have to make sure that her medical records will say that her injury may cause her mind to become in a mental state, when she starts her revenge rampage; I know it's coming. Should I say that she is schizophrenic? No Nita, just wait, calm down, take some deep breaths, focus on your girls, and get it together!"

Getting back to the conversation with Aaron and Officer Harrison.

"Not yet, sir, it was no trouble at all. I have children myself and I am really sorry for what happened to your daughters. We are still here at the school asking questions. We found the pipe that was used to hit one of your daughters and we have a witness who saw the person slashing the tires." Then Officer Harrison said, "Hold one minute," as he talked with another officer.

Aaron could hear the conversation, as the other officer said, "They just found the razor that cut the girl's neck."

Officer Harrison said, "Where was it found?"

"The men's room trash can," the other officer said.

Then Officer Harrison said, "Officer Bailey, can you see if you can get a little more from the witness who saw the person slash the tires?"

"Will do, sir," Officer Bailey said.

Officer Harrison said, "Sorry for keeping you on hold for that length of time, that was one of the other officers coming to tell me-"

Aaron cut Officer Harrison off. "I heard every word loud and clear," he said. "You know, Officer Harrison, my girls have been bullied ever since they were in elementary school."

Officer Harrison said, "Oh really, is that so? Can you explain that to me?"

Aaron said, "Officer Harrison, my wife and I work really hard for our family. I wasn't even 30 years old when we had our quads. My girls are smart. They have been A students throughout school. They speak four foreign languages fluently. They are pretty. They hold black belts in karate. They run track daily and they are excellent gymnasts. There's no doubt in my mind, if my girls had seen their attacker or attackers coming, they would have given them a go for their time. Right now, my mind is all over the place. I need to have their car towed to the shop. Have they completed the investigation on the car? (Aaron took a heavy sigh.) I should be inside with my girls. Officer Harrison, is there any way we can meet, like at my office tomorrow? And when the tow truck comes to pick up the car, will you please assist him?"

"Sure, I will. We've dusted the car for fingerprints and taken pictures of the damage. We will have everything tested to see if the object that was used to cut the back of your daughter's neck is the same object that was used to cut the tires. Don't worry, I'm not going anywhere for a while. I am off tomorrow. I'll be more than happy to meet with you. Let me get the address," said Officer Harrison.

"The address is 1512 Parker Avenue, Suite 308; that's in Tampa," Aaron said.

"Ok, I got it. That's 1512 Parker Avenue, Suite 308 in Tampa. Will 10:00 a.m. be ok?" Officer Harrison said.

"10 o'clock sounds great. I'll see you then, and Officer Harrison, I thank you again," Aaron said.

"Oh, no problem. Another officer is talking with the dean now. I hope when we meet, I will have more that I can tell you about this case, like catching this fool or these fools who did this," said Officer Harrison.

"Thank you again, goodbye," Aaron said.

Aaron walked back into the hospital, putting the business card back into his pocket. Then he called his insurance company to let them know that he needed a tow truck sent to the girls' school. As he paced the floor, Aaron told the insurance company that the car may have yellow tape around it and asked the driver to look for Officer Harrison. The insurance agent gathered all the necessary information and told Aaron that a truck would be out within 45 minutes to one hour.

Aaron sat down and Anita came out to talk with them. She hugged Ebony and Destiny and said, "I'm so glad the both of you are ok."

Anita told them, "Christian is being stitched up right now, but she's in a lot of pain. Erin is receiving blood. The area where the nurse shaved her head, the doctor noticed that the spot is very tender. She is now sedated while they run multiple tests; they want to make sure that her skull is not fractured. (Anita started to bat her eyes really fast.) My babies are really hurt."

When Anita said that, tears started to form in her eyes. Aaron hugged her and told her, "It's going to be ok!"

"I know that it will be. I'm just sad right now," Anita said.

"I'm not going to sit back and let whoever do whatever they think is ok and get away with it. Noooo no, not today," Aaron said.

Anita got herself together and she said, "Christian is alert. She was given pain medication. Come on, let me take you back so that you can see them and keep them company. They are in separate rooms right now. I'm sure they are going to be admitted tonight. I'll make sure that they will be in a room together."

So they went back in the examining area. The girls' eyes were filled with tears.

Anita said, "Don't cry, they will be ok. Just let them know that you are here. Now Christian is laying on her stomach because the gash on the back of her neck was so close to her spine. They are keeping her still. You will have to raise the bed in order for her to see you, or you can sit down on the stool and look up at her. She might be in and out, but just talk to her. Just keep in mind if she talks out of her head, remember it's the medication."

As they walked into the room where Christian was, the girls kissed her on her head, and Aaron got down on the floor and looked up at Chris. He called her name and said, "Hey, Chris."

She responded by saying, "Hey, Daddy."

Then Aaron said, "How do you feel?"

Chris said, "I feel alright."

"Do you know why you are in the hospital?" Aaron asked.

"Yes, I do, Daddy. I was walking past the men's bathroom when someone came from behind me and cut me on the back of my neck. I felt a sting and then something wet. When I put my hand on my neck, that's when I saw that it was blood. I started putting pressure to it and then I started getting dizzy. I could hear the alarm sounding off, but I couldn't say anything. I could see people running in the hall and I heard someone say, 'Oh my God, we have another one,' and after that, I don't remember anything," Christian said.

"You must have passed out. How are you feeling right now, baby girl?" Aaron said.

"My head and my neck are starting to hurt again, Daddy. I just want to sleep," Chris said.

"Let me get someone in here to give you more pain medicine, Chris.

Can you push that button so someone will come? I could tell that you were starting to feel pain again. I can see it in your face," Aaron said.

Then Anita said, "I'm right here; someone is coming. Let's give Chris some time to rest. She's going to be out of it for a while. We'll come back later. Erin is across the hall and two rooms down."

They walked down the hall to Erin's room. Aaron walked in first. Anita yelled, "Oh my God! (She stopped and looked up the hall.) Room 7 stat!"

The doctors ran down the hall to the room that Erin was in. Anita ran inside. Erin was having a seizure. Oh God, please help my child. Help my baby, Father. She needs you. We need you right now."

Anita started working on Erin, as the medical staff ran into the room around Aaron. Ebony and Destiny were standing looking, with tears in their eyes.

The doctor told Anita, "Step aside, Dr. Jackson, we can take over."

They put medication into Erin's IV line and the seizure started to calm down. A doctor asked the family if they would step out of the room, and they did. A few minutes later, they ran down the hall pushing Erin's bed. They let the family know that she was going for an MRI test to see if bleeding or fluid was building up on her brain.

When that was said, Anita fell to her knees, then Aaron went down with her, then Ebony and Destiny, and they prayed. Aaron prayed loudly, "Heavenly Father, we come to you just as we are, weak. But God we know that you are our strength. Lord, we raised our children in the church. They know your Word, from Genesis to Revelation. You are our help, our anchor in this storm that we are going through. Right now, Father, this is one we can't handle. My babies and your children need you right now. Right now, Father. You said you are a doctor for the doctors. I need you to go with them, guide, and direct them, as they do all that is needed to help my children. I know that you said, you will never leave us nor forsake us. We are leaning and depending on your most Holy and Righteous Word. We declare and decree healing in Jesus' name. By your stripes, Erin and Christian Jackson are healed. Amen, and thank you, God."

And then everyone said, "Amen." Aaron was so loud when he prayed that a patient in one of the other rooms also said, "Amen."

When they stood up, Aaron said, "She will be ok. Our Father, who art in Heaven, got it all in control. He will show you."

Aaron winked his eye at them. With a smile, he said, "I'm ok now. I just took it to the Cross. I can go home, get ready for tomorrow, and wait for the call saying that Erin is improving.

"Baby, you have been here for more than 12 hours, you can't do anything, we just did it all. Now let go and let God take control. We're going to let them take Christian to her room and then we are all going to go home."

Aaron's phone rang. He answered it and said, "Attorney Jackson speaking." The voice on the other end was Officer Harrison.

"Mr. Jackson, the witness who saw the person cutting the tires, carries a camera with him at all times. He has pictures of the maniac who slashed the tires. We have the negatives and we promised him once we develop the film, we will give him all the other pictures. This boy really is an authentic nerd. Look, I know you are with your family. I wanted to give you an update. We'll meet in the morning!"

"That is great news, Officer Harrison, I look forward to meeting with you. You have a good night," Aaron said.

Tyrone, an orderly, came down and walked over to Anita and told her, "Dr. Jackson, I am here to take Christian up to her room. I need you to sign off on the transfer."

He passed the clipboard to Anita and she looked over the papers.

"Ok, Tyrone. So, Chris will be taken to room 206, correct? Is that a single room or does it have two beds?"

"Yes, room 206 has two beds. I know you didn't think they were going to separate your daughters, did you?" Tyrone said.

"I'm just making sure," Anita said.

Anita signed off on the papers and handed the clipboard back to Tyrone. The family walked down the hall to the room that Christian was in. She was still sleeping.

"Oh, Tyrone, the bed that Christian is on now is the bed that will stay in room 206 until tomorrow. You do know that, correct?"

"Yes ma'am, I do," Tyrone said.

"Before we go, let me check on Erin. Then we can run up to Chris's room, and we will be ready to go home," Anita said.

Anita walked over to the phone and called radiology.

"Hi, Pam, this is Nurse Jackson," Anita said.

"Everyone's calling you Dr. Jackson," Pam said.

Anita said, "I noticed that. Yes, it will be official in three days. Look, are all the testing completed on Erin?"

"Yes, they are," Pam said.

"Can you read to me the findings?" Anita said.

"Sure, hold one moment, while I get the chart," Pam said.

Pam placed Anita on hold, then she came back to the phone and said, "Dr. Jackson, it looks like a small amount of fluid is on Erin's brain. A tube has been inserted to drain the fluid. The tests showed that's what caused her seizure. Would you like me to see where she is now?"

"If you would please, thank you," Anita said.

Anita was placed on hold again. While she was holding, she told the family what was going on and then Pam came back to the phone.

"Dr. Jackson, Erin is being transported to ICU-7, right now," Pam said.

"Pam, I thank you for your help. You have a good night," Anita said.

"You try and have a good night as well, Dr. Jackson. Try not to worry, God is in control. So don't worry, your girls will be fine," Pam said.

"I know they will. I've already turned it over to the Master. Thank you, I've got to go. Good night," Anita said.

After their call ended, Anita turned to her family and said, "Ok, they had to insert a tube into Erin's head to drain the fluid off. That's what caused her seizure. They are taking her to the intensive care unit, so that she is monitored throughout the night. Let's go see her. Chris, this has been a long day. I am glad I am off tomorrow."

As they walked down the hall, Aaron said, "Ebony and Destiny, you know you won't be going to school tomorrow. First thing in the morning, I'm going to get cellular phones for everybody in the house. If you can't do anything else, you can dial 911. Then I'm meeting with the officer who brought both of you here. It has been a long day. I'm hungry and I am so glad we have leftovers. Just warm it up."

"I really don't want to go back," Destiny said.

"There are only a few weeks to go before all of you graduate. You know that your dad is going to make sure you all are ok," Anita said.

"You got that right. If I have to take off from my job and go from room to room with you, then I will. But that is one thing I will discuss with the school and Officer Harrison on tomorrow," Aaron said.

They were now on the elevator going up to the first floor where the intensive care unit was. The elevator stopped. They got off and walk towards the ICU. When the nurse on that unit saw Anita, she pointed to the room that Erin was in and said, "The doctors are with your daughter now."

Anita said to her family, "Wait. Let me make sure it's ok for all of us to come in."

Anita walked behind the curtains. One of the doctors turned and looked at Anita. His name was Dr. Ralph Franklin.

"We notice some improvement already," Dr. Franklin said. "We'll just monitor Erin throughout the night and make sure that there's no swelling, bleeding, or any more buildup of fluid. We're going to keep her heavily sedated until the tubing is removed in the morning. You go home and get some rest. I'll be here. She'll be ok."

"I know she will," Anita said, as she looked over at Erin. "Dr. Franklin, I am exhausted, both mentally and physically. I thank you for caring for my baby. I couldn't ask for a better physician and I feel good about that. But before we go, my family just want to give Erin a kiss good night."

"Oh sure, why did you leave them outside?" Dr. Franklin said.

"I didn't know what was being administered to Erin and I didn't know if my girls could take seeing that," Anita said.

Anita walked over to the curtain and pulled it back. She told her family to come in. "We are only going to stay for a second," she said.

As Erin laid there with tubes connected to her, Aaron walked beside the bed and told her, "Baby girl, God is in control. By His stripes, you are healed. I love you and I'll see you tomorrow."

Then Destiny went over to the other side of the bed and touched Erin on the shoulder and said, "I love you, Erin."

Aaron walked to the foot of the bed and Ebony walked over to the head of the bed and she told Erin, "Feel better soon, sister. We have graduation coming. I love you."

Then Aaron walked over to Erin and said, "I love you, sweet pea. I'll see you in the morning."

After the family left the ICU, they headed to the next floor to visit with Christian. When they got to her room, she was awake and she smiled when her family entered the room. The bed was raised to where she was almost standing.

Anita walked into the room and said, "Well, look at you, now that's what you call sleeping standing up. How's my baby feeling?"

"I'm ok, my head isn't hurting right now and it's probably because I was given medication not long ago," Chris said.

"Hi, Daddy, did we talk earlier? It seems like you asked me what happened at school," Chris said.

"Yes, we did, pumpkin. You were out of it. But you did talk to me with your eyes closed and then the pain became unbearable. They gave you more medication and then you fell asleep," Aaron answered.

"Hey, Ebony and Des, where's Erin?" Christian asked.

Anita walked over to Chris and explained, "You have been out of it for a while. Erin was hurt today also. She was brought here by ambulance the same time you were. She was hit in the back of her head and her injury is more serious than yours. Right now, she is in the intensive care unit, but we are hoping that tomorrow she will be right there in that bed. (Anita pointed to the other bed.) The doctors want to observe her for the night. Don't you worry about anything, just focus on getting better."

"Chris, your mom, your sisters, and I are getting sleepy. It has been a rough day. I am happy to see that you are alert and you're able to stay up longer. That means you are getting better. You get some rest and we will see you tomorrow. Ok, pumpkin?" Aaron said.

"Ok, Daddy. I know that God is watching over Erin and me. After that prayer that you prayed, that was you who was praying so loud? I think I said, 'Amen,' but somewhere out in the hall I heard someone say, 'Amen,' and then I fell asleep," Chris said.

With a smile on his face, Aaron replied, "Yes, it was me praying loudly, as you say. You know I got to send my timber up."

"Y'all go on home. My head is starting to hurt, but not like it was earlier. I think I need something for the pain. I love y'all, and I will see you tomorrow. I want to go to sleep," Chris said.

They all told Chris that they loved her and blew kisses at her as they left the room. A nurse came down the hall with the medication to put in Christian's IV tube.

Holly said, "Hi, Dr. Jackson, I was just on my way to give Christian her pain medication. I'm sorry to hear about your daughters, but you know they are in good hands."

"I know they are. That's why my family and I can go home and get some rest. We've been here all evening and we are going home right now. You have a good night, Holly," Anita said.

"Good night, Dr. Jackson," Holly said.

It was eleven o'clock p.m. when the Jacksons headed home. The girls decided that one would ride home with their mother, while the other would ride with their father.

When they got home, they all were so tired. The only thing they could do was sit down.

Aaron said, "If I sit too long, I'm going to fall asleep. I'm hungry and I have a busy day tomorrow. Honey, pass me the remote, please. I want to see the news before I turn in. Let me go wash my hands and eat while I watch TV."

When Aaron got up, they all got up to wash. While eating and watching the news, the incident at the school was shown. They did not have many details, but Erin's and Christian's names were mentioned. The reporter did say that the story was still unfolding and that a possible witness may have seen something. Also, the dean of the school was interviewed.

"Unfolding, oh, it's going to unfold. I am going to get to the bottom of this madness. Let me finish my food so I can go to bed. Get some sleep; it's going to be a long day. (Then Aaron looked at the girls.) School is closed for the both of you until I find security for you. Call or send your professors an email for your assignments," Aaron said.

Aaron stood up, drank his water, gave a belch, and said, "Good night, I love you. See you in the morning."

When the morning came, Aaron got up, took his shower, got dressed, and kissed his bride. When he kissed Anita, it woke her up and she looked at the clock and said, "Good morning honey, you are up and dressed already. Did you eat?"

"I don't have time to eat. I have a very busy day. I need to get everyone in the house their cellular phones first. Then, I'm going to check on the car. And after that, I am going to the office and meet with Officer Harrison. He's the officer who gave the girls a ride to the hospital. We have a lot to discuss. After that, I'm going over to the school. Then, I'll be going by the hospital," he said.

"If the car is ready, call me so that the girls and I can pick it up before we go over to the hospital," Anita said.

"What time you plan to go to the hospital?" Aaron asked.

"I plan to go around 1:00. We didn't get any calls, so no news is good news," Aaron said.

"You know how God works. You felt it deep down that the girls will be ok. I wasn't expecting a call, were you?" Aaron said.

"Nope, I have to call our family. I know they are worried. None of us talked with any of them yesterday," Anita said.

"I've got to run and get started. I'll call Junior and I'll call you after my meeting with the officer, love you. Please make sure that you call our family," Aaron said.

"I love you, talk with you later," Anita answered.

As Aaron walked out of the bedroom, Anita turned over and went back to sleep.

Aaron made his first stop at the auto shop. He got out of his car, walked inside, and said, "Morning Mike, is my girls' car ready?"

"Oh, morning to you, AJ. No, it's not ready yet. I'm waiting for my tire shipment to come in. He should have been here by now. Maybe he's stuck in traffic. But when the tires are unloaded, your car will be the first one that we get to. Hey, I saw the news last night about what happened at the school. It's a damn shame. What is this world coming to? Are the girls ok?" Mike asked.

"Yeah, they got hurt pretty bad. They are still in the hospital. When the police catch who did this, oh, you know they are going to pay. I don't care who they are. Not because it's my girls, but who's thinking of craziness like that. Then you go commit the act to another human being, interrupting the entire school. Now you have people on edge. Mike, I'd better shut up, I can feel myself boiling inside. I will have my day in court with them. You can take that to the bank!" Aaron said.

"AJ, I'll call you when the car is ready," Mike said.

"That sounds good. Oh, better yet, give Nita a call. She's at home today. How much is it going to cost? Let me pay for it now," Aaron said.

"Ok cool," Mike said.

Mike went over to the adding machine and started calculating, and then he said to Aaron, "It's going to be three hundred dollars."

Aaron handed his card to Mike and said, "That way, when Nita comes, she won't have to bother with paying. Hey look, thanks again. I've got to run," Aaron said.

"Talk with you later," Mike said.

Aaron got into his car, drove off, and headed to the phone store. When he arrived, he got out the car and went into the store. One of the sales reps walked over to him and said, "Good morning, sir. I'm Isaiah, how may I help you?"

"Well, I'm looking to purchase five phones," Aaron said.

"Is there any particular phone you are looking for?" Isaiah asked.

"No special phone in particular. One that rings and makes calls. This is the phone I have. It's a flip phone," Aaron answered.

Then the rep said, "Oh, you have one of our flip phones. They are right over here."

They walked over to the phone display. The rep said, "They come in many colors. Is there any specific color that you are looking for?"

"Well, now that I see all the different colors, I'll just get five phones each a different color. That way there won't be any mix-up," Aaron said.

"Ok, good. Let me go into the back and get the phones. I will meet you at the counter!" Isaiah said.

When the sales rep came back with the phones, he got all the necessary information that he needed from Aaron. Then he assigned a phone number to each phone.

After the transaction was completed, Isaiah said, "Mr. Jackson, is there anything else I can help you with today?"

"No, I think I have what I need right now. Thanks for your help,"

Aaron said.

"Oh, no problem, glad I could help. You have a good day," the sales rep said.

Aaron turned and walked away. "You do the same," he said.

Aaron walked out the store. He put the shopping bag in the trunk of his car and headed to the office.

When he got to the office and walked in, he said, "Good morning," to Angie, the receptionist.

"Attorney Jackson, I'm so sorry to hear what happened to Erin and Chris. Are they ok? Oh, and good morning to you, sir," Angie said.

"They are both still in the hospital. Nita and the girls are going to visit with them today. I'm going to see them when I finish here. Did I get a call from an Officer Harrison?" Aaron said.

"No sir, but here are your other calls. Most of them are from your family," Angie said.

"Let me go look over these and answer as many as I can before the officer arrives. When he gets here, I don't want to be disturbed," Aaron said.

"Ok, Attorney Jackson," Angie said.

Aaron walked down the hall and he had tons of messages on his phone. He listened to them and most of the calls were family from out of town calling with concerns about the girls.

Attorney Jackson answered his messages and returned some of his clients' calls. Most were advising them on what not to do or say. Then his intercom announced that Officer Harrison was waiting to see him. Aaron walked out of his office and down the hall to greet him. They greeted each other with a handshake and then a man hug.

Then Aaron said, "Officer Harrison, come on down to my office."

While they walked down the hall, Officer Harrison said, "I have a lot to talk about."

They walked into the office and Aaron closed the door behind them.

He said, "Have a seat, Officer Harrison."

And then Officer Harrison said, "This is going to be a long process when everything unfolds. We will be calling each other by first names. By the way, I'm Jeffery, most people call me Jeff. You know, I feel like I'm wearing your shoes. I have children."

"Well, I'm Aaron. Anyone who showed concern like you have is alright with me. Thanks, Jeff. So what you got for me?" Aaron said.

"Well, you see these folders. These are copies of all that was done last night, all of the witnesses, everything that we have compiled so far. First, let me say, it's a shame you can't even send your children to school to get their education. I speak this way because my daughter was accepted into the school starting in the fall, which is only a few months away. It makes me wonder if I will let her go or not. And on the joking side, when I looked into my rearview mirror yesterday, while driving your girls to the hospital, I noticed they are identical," Jeffery said.

"Yes, they all are. We can identify them because one has a mole on her face, the other has thicker eyebrows, one has a birthmark on her neck, and the other one doesn't have any of those identifying marks. If it wasn't for that, my wife and I would have been messed up," Aaron said.

"So, you have identical quads?" Jeff asked.

"Yes, we do," Aaron answered.

"Now let's get right into this business, Aaron. We arrested a student at 3:00 a.m. this morning. We went to his house and got him out of his bed. The judge did not grant a bond. His family is furious. They are holding him, a white boy. You have to thank that photographer. This boy is sharp. We have pictures of the clothes the guy was wearing, each side of his face, his height, that Mohawk haircut, and the tattoo on his hand. I'm happy about that," Jeff said.

"Mohawk, would his name happen to be Peter Pitts?" Aaron asked.

Jeff had a shocked look on his face as he said, "Yes, it is. How did you know this?"

"Oh my God, Jeff, you won't believe this," Aaron said. "My girls told me a few weeks ago that they saw two of those clowns at the school! Let me go back. My wife and I, along with our children, lived in D.C. These boys harassed and bullied my girls in elementary school. I tried to walk the straight and narrow, but my girls beat those boys' asses just before graduation. I met with each one of those boys at the school myself, and the principal. I recorded every word that was said out their mouths, these idiots!

"I typed word for word what was said in the meeting and printed it out on paper what these sick minded individuals said as children. I have the papers and the tape in my file cabinet. I am going to use everything I have in court. You know, I believe it was one of them who blew a blow dart and hit my daughter Destiny on the leg when the girls walked to their car, leaving school."

"So what you are telling me is this nightmare followed your girls all the way from D.C. to Florida?" Jeff said.

"I don't know, I'd like to think that this school was the best for their major, but they are not enrolled in the school. I'm not understanding how this can be. They came this far and all these years passed by. Now they are showing up again. They came to get my girls, and they are all going to rot in hell. You watch what I tell you!" Aaron said.

"Well, let me tell you, the judge is a very close friend to my family, both she and her husband. She's tough. This thing about whites beating blacks, oh, that's not going to fly in her court. You watch what I tell you. I don't care how much that boy's parent pays for his attorney, they will be wasting their money. I'm going to have dinner at my house. I want you and your wife to come, and I'll invite Freda; that's the judge's name. Her husband's name is Samuel Perkins. I'll let my wife Kendra know and we will set a day," Jeff said.

Meanwhile, back at the Jackson's home, Anita and the girls were up. It was around 12:30 in the afternoon and the phone rang. It was Aaron Jr. calling. When Anita answered the phone, you could hear the nervousness in his voice.

Anita said, "Hello."

"Mom, it's me Junior, what happened? I was on the computer listening to the local news, the tragedy at the school aired. What happened, Ma?"

Anita said, "Erin and Christian were injured at school. Erin was hit in the back of the head with a pipe. She lost a lot of blood. She fell and was laying in the hall until someone found her and went for help. She's in intensive care right now, fluid buildup on her brain. So the doctors had to insert a tube to drain the fluid. Chris was cut on the back of her neck and needed lots of stitches. She is in a lot of pain. The doctors are giving her antibiotics and medication for the pain. When we all left the hospital last night, Chris was feeling somewhat better. Her pain level has subsided to the point where she could talk to us and she did not need medication as often, but Erin was heavily sedated."

"But did the police catch the person who did this?" Aaron Jr. asked.

"Not to my knowledge. Your dad is meeting with one of the officers who was called on the scene yesterday, right now at his office!" Anita explained.

"Do I need to come home now, Mama?" Junior asked.

"No, you are scheduled to be home soon for the girls' graduation. If we need you, we know how to get in contact with you," Anita said.

"Are you sure?" Junior said.

"Yes, I am, Junior. It's nothing you can do right now but just pray," Anita said.

"Ok, let me call Daddy. Kiss my sisters for me and tell them I'll see them soon, and when Erin is alert tell her I said clock it," he said.

"Do I really need to tell her that? You know your sister. She is not going to let this go. Look, call your dad, and I'll talk with you soon. I love you, bye," Anita said.

Back at the attorney's office. "That sounds like a plan. Just let me know when and Nita and I will be there. If there's anything you want us to bring, just let us know," Aaron said.

"You won't have to bring a thing; cooking is what my wife loves. You know the restaurant Kendra Taste, Exquisite Cuisine? We own that," Jeff said.

"Oh yes, I know it well. My wife and I love Kendra Taste. It's pricy, but that doesn't stop us. Why not meet there? That way the workers can clean and we can meet in one of the private rooms." Aaron said.

"Ok, let's get back to nailing these jokers," Aaron said.

Then the phone rang. Aaron said, "Sorry, give me one minute. I asked my receptionist to hold all my calls. If she let this one go through, it must be important."

Aaron answered the phone and said, "Good afternoon, Attorney Jackson speaking."

"Hey, Daddy," Aaron Jr. said.

"Hey, son, how are you?" Aaron Sr. said.

"I'm good. I just talked with Mom and she briefed me on what happened. I saw it on the news," Junior said.

"Yeah, a real live mess. I don't know what these boys have on their minds, but I'm getting ready to give them something to think about,"

Aaron said.

"What boys?" Junior asked.

"Oh, that's right. I haven't told your mom yet. I have Officer Jeffery Harrison here in my office. One of the boys was arrested this morning, and son, you won't believe it's Peter Pitts," Aaron said.

"Ok, Dad. Who is Peter Pitts?" Junior said.

"Peter Pitts is one of those punks that was bullying your sisters in the sixth grade. Don't you remember you wanted to come to their school with me, and Erin told you, 'No, what could you do about it?'" Aaron said.

"I don't remember the names, but the sixth grade, Dad? The same guy attacked my sisters after all these years. They really want to hurt them. So what are you going to do about it, Daddy?" Junior asked.

"Well, Jeff and I are working on some things. Your sisters are not going back to school without security. I don't care what the school says. Someone will be with them until they graduate," Aaron said.

"You're losing me, Dad. You said boys. Is there more than one?" Junior asked.

Aaron said, "I believe there is and that's one of the things we are looking into right now. Your sisters saw Peter Pitts and Bobby Spinks at the school over a month ago and they haven't seen them anymore. But that's not puzzling to me; that's how snakes sliver. And these boys are not enrolled in the school.

"One second, son. (Aaron put Junior on speaker phone.) Jeff, I have to give you the names of the other boys when I get off the phone. We are going to run a search on these names and find out if they are all living here in Florida. Son, let me get back with you. Oh, I bought cellular phones for everyone in the house. Call tonight, we should be home around 10 o'clock, so then you can get the numbers and the updates on everything!"

"Ok, Dad, if no one answers the home phone, I will call you on your cell phone. I love you, Daddy, talk with you later," Junior said.

"I love you too, son, talk with you later," Aaron said.

"Thanks, Jeff. Let's get back to where we left off. Now, you heard what I said to my son. The other boys' names are Richard Rivers, Billy Goldstein, and Bobby Spinks. See if we can find out where these punks live. I need to have stay away orders issued for each one of them and I want to know the other schools they attended from elementary up till now. We need to know the character of each one of these monkeys. I want the judge to put out a subpoena for their medical records and school records. I think I need to meet with Judge Freda sooner than later. Jeff, can you make it happen?" Aaron said.

"I think I can. How soon do you want to meet?" Jeff asked.

"If this Saturday is good for everyone, let's make it happen," Aaron said.

"Well, ok then, we're going to get this ball rolling. Speaking of ball, how about us getting together and do full court, run a few games, burn off some of that stress, like Saturday morning; I'll let some of my officer buddies know," Jeff said.

"Cool, I'm gamed, and I'll call a couple of my buddies and we'll just have a good time," Aaron said.

"I know you want security for your girls. When is this going to start?" Jeff asked.

"I need to talk with my girls and find out how their day flows with their schedules," Aaron said.

"Look, I have a few brothers on the force who work with me from time to time and they tell me how some of these white police officers are towards blacks. Right now, they are not working 12-hour days like I am, and I'm sure they wouldn't mind looking out for your girls on their off days. Now don't get me wrong, a lot of our people are their own worst enemy, and some of them just don't want to do right. But the chief is white and that makes the other whites feel superior over the blacks, and he allows this. There's a lot that goes on and no one is talking. That's why I volunteer sometimes at the youth center. Our black people really need to be educated on life's ups and downs. And when I get with those boys, I do and see good results from the work that they do. This song always pops in my head, "*If I Can Help Somebody*." I stand on those words. I don't want to live my life in vain. I love helping others. That's why I'm going to have my boys and I protect and watch over you girls while they are at school," Jeff said.

"I am humbled and grateful for meeting you. After you talk with them, have them to give me a call. We can discuss a fee," Aaron said.

"A fee, did you say a fee? Man, you don't know how many working people who can't even afford a lawyer. If they are there for you at no cost, wouldn't you do the same in return?" Jeff asked.

"Oh, of course, without a doubt. God didn't bless me with this business here and in South Carolina, by beating people out of their money. Now I did hear you say that they are not getting the hours that you are. So once we talk, I'll see what they say, and that includes a fee for you too, Jeff!" Aaron said.

"Well, alright then, I'll give them a call and have them to call you. After you talk with the people at the school, just let me know when your girls are going back to school. In the meantime, I will set up that dinner date," Jeff said.

"Hey, Jeff, like I said, I'm glad we met today. I am going to run over to the school. Oh, let me make copies of the meeting that I had with the principal at the elementary school where this mess started. What was his name? (Aaron pondered for a bit trying to remember.) Oh, that's right, Mr. Stonewall; his name was Mr. Stonewall. I was not playing then and I surely am not playing now. I'm going to find out what's going on," Aaron said.

"Why don't I come along with you? I'll bring my recorder and pad for notes. Who knows? Two heads are better than one, and while they are holding that one guy, I'm sure you may be getting court papers to appear soon," Jeff said.

"Great, I need the support. I hope something is in the mail. I need to get these stay away orders done quickly!" Aaron said.

Back at the Jackson's home, after Anita's call with Junior was over, Anita called Mike at the mechanic shop.

"Good afternoon, Mike, this is Nita, Aaron's wife!"

"Oh, yes, Nita, the car is ready," Mike said.

"Oh, good, I'll be there shortly," Nita said.

After Nita hung up the phone, she yelled upstairs to the girls, "Ebony and Des, come on, I'm ready to leave. The car is ready. I want to get over to the hospital early, so that we can get home earlier than last night."

"Destiny said, "We're coming, Mom."

When Ebony and Destiny came down the stairs and said that they were ready, Anita said, "Junior called. He saw what happened at the school online. He wanted to come home, but I know that his tour will be over soon. I assured him that everything will be ok. He told me to kiss all of his sisters and to tell you that he loves you and that he will see you soon."

Then Anita went over and kissed both girls, one on each cheek, and she said, "One kiss is for Junior, and the other is for me. Come on, do you have everything?"

Ebony said, "Yes."

And then Destiny said, "I have everything."

"Oh, before we leave, let me call your dad and see how things went today with the officer," Anita said.

She walked over to the phone and dialed Aaron's work number. Angie answered the phone, "Good afternoon, Jackson Law Firm. This is Angie, how may I help you?"

"Hi, Angie, this is Mrs. Jackson. Is Mr. Jackson available?"

Angie stuttered, "Hold, hold one second, let me catch him."

Angie placed the phone on hold and ran to catch Aaron; he just closed the office door heading outside.

"Mr. Jackson," Angie yelled. "Mrs. Jackson is on the phone."

"Tell her I'll call her at home in one minute," Aaron said.

"Ok sir, I will," Angie said.

Angie went back into the office, picked up the phone, and said, "Mrs. Jackson, Mr. Jackson said he will call you in one minute. Oh, Mrs. Jackson, I told Mr. Jackson this morning, I am sorry to hear what happened to Erin and Christian. I prayed for both of them."

"Thanks, Angie. I know you love them. I will let them know that you send your love. You have a wonderful day, goodbye," Anita said.

Anita hung up the phone with Angie and did not have the chance to take her hand off the phone when it started to ring. She picked it up. It was Aaron calling.

Anita answered, "Hi, honey."

And then Aaron said, "How did you know that it was me?"

"Well, you normally do what you say. How did things go with the officer?" Anita said.

"The meeting went well. They got Peter Pitts, one of the boys who harassed the girls in elementary school. The judge ordered that he will be held until court. Jeffery is the officer's name, but he prefers to be called Jeff. And would you believe that the judge is close friends with him and his wife Kendra? We are trying to set up a dinner date so that we can meet with them at Kendra Taste this Saturday. It's going to be Jeff and his wife, his officer buddies and their wives, the judge, and her husband!" Aaron said.

"Wonderful, that is awesome news. I can't believe that monster came all the way to Florida and attends the same school our children attend. But, I am happy to know that he won't be on the streets to bully them for now. What about the other guy that the girls saw?" Nita asked.

"I am on my way up to the school right now, Jeff and me. We are going to find out about all of that!" Aaron said.

"Saturday will be good. We needed to meet like a month ago," Nita said.

"I have a lot to talk about when we get home, so I'll see you when I come to the hospital. Love you," Aaron said.

"Love you too," Nita said.

So they left the house and headed to the shop to pick up the car. While driving to the shop, Ebony said, "Mom, who got arrested?"

"Peter Pitts is in jail and being held without bond for now. The officer who brought the both of you to the hospital knows the judge. Dad is going to tell me the rest when we get home. He's on his way to the school with Jeff, the officer," Anita said.

Ebony and Destiny gave each other a high five, and Ebony said, "I told you, sis, we ran over to the right officer. Boy, I am glad I was thinking."

"I'm glad you were, too. I'll be happy when this is all over. I am tired of having to look over my shoulder again. I thought that this was in the past, and now the devil strikes again," Destiny said.

"I rebuke the devil, in the name of Jesus. Satan, you can't have my children," Anita said.

Now that the car was picked up, Ebony and Destiny rode together and Anita told them, "I want you to get in front of me and I will follow."

They arrived at the hospital and they went up to the intensive care unit first. Deborah was the nurse sitting at the nurses' station when she saw Anita and the girls.

She said, "Hi, Dr. Jackson, Erin was taken down to room 206 with Christian early this morning!"

"Oh, no one called me," Anita said.

"Well, Dr. Franklin was going to call to let you know, but then he said he would only call if there was an emergency. And Erin is improving," Deborah said.

As Anita threw up her hands, she said, "Hallelujah, God! I thank you! Come on, let's go up and see my babies. Thanks, Deb."

Meanwhile, Aaron and Jeff were at the school. They got out of the car and walked around the parking lot. Jeff pointed and said, "That's where your girls' car was parked, and right over there is where the student was taking his pictures. Come on, let's go in, so that I can take you to where both girls were found. You know, I wonder what was the time frame between both incidents. They happened on different floors and we only have one guy in custody."

"Let's go inside and talk with whomever we can get to talk," Aaron said.

As Aaron and Jeff walked up the steps to go into the building, Jeff said,

"I hope we can get something out of the dean bat, dean. The officer who interviewed him said that he was in total shock and all he could say is, 'Nothing like this ever happened at this school as long as I've been the dean.' And get this, his name is Dean. You get Dean Dean; it stands for ding ding; that's how he appeared."

Then Elroy, the student who took the pictures was coming out of the building, when Jeff said, "Hey, Elroy, do you remember me?"

"No, I'm afraid I don't!" Elroy said.

"That's ok. You probably don't, but I'm Officer Harrison. I talked with you yesterday. I want to thank you for those great pictures that you took. (Jeff reached down into his briefcase, pulled out an envelope, and extended his arm to pass it to Elroy.) These are the other pictures that were on the negatives. Thank you, and let me introduce you. This is Mr. Jackson. He's the father of the girls that were involved in the tragic incident."

Elroy appeared to be shy. He didn't make eye contact with Jeff or Aaron, but he did look up for a short second to take his pictures.

Aaron extended his hand to shake Elroy's hand.

"Elroy, I want to thank you for the good work that you did. You've helped the officers and my family a whole lot. Here's my business card; if I can help you in any way, just call me," Aaron said.

"Ok," Elroy said, as he walked away.

When Elroy walked away, Aaron and Jeff looked at each other wondering what was up with him. Then they heard Elroy say something. They stopped and turned around.

"Elroy, can you repeat what you just said?" Jeff said, as they walked down a few steps towards him.

"I said Christian is my friend. Who would want to hurt her?" he said.

"I know, Elroy. She is in the hospital getting better. If you know anything about what happened, please, do it for your friend. Help her if you can and we will do everything we can to see that you get a job in your photography field," Jeff said.

Elroy looked up at the both of them that time and said, "Would you really do that for me?"

"Yes, we will, Elroy," Aaron said.

"Can I call you on this number?" Elroy asked.

"Yes, anytime!" Aaron said.

"Here's my card, Elroy. If you can't reach Mr. Jackson, try calling me," Jeff said.

"Oh thanks, tell Christian I'm sorry for what happened to her," Elroy said, as he ran down the steps.

"You think he knows more than he's telling us?" Jeff asked Aaron.

"I kind of picked that up also. We need to see if Elroy is going to give us a call," Aaron said.

"Well, if he doesn't call you or me, we just have to pay Elroy another visit," Jeff said.

"I think he's going to tell us something. You see how he looked at us when we talked about what he's most passionate about?" Aaron said.

"Yes, I did," Jeff said, as they walked into the school.

The first stop was at Mr. Dean's office. The receptionist's desk was just as you walked into the office. Both Aaron and Jeff stopped at the desk.

Aaron said, "Good afternoon, I am Aaron Jackson, the father of Erin and Christian Jackson. This is Officer Harrison. We would like to have a brief meeting with Mr. Dean."

"Sure, one minute, while I let him know that you're here," the receptionist said.

So the receptionist called Mr. Dean to inform him that guests were in the office to see him. He informed her that he would be out shortly.

"He will be right out. Would you like to have a seat?" she said to the guests.

"No thanks, I'll stand. If I sit and Mr. Dean comes right out, then I'll be getting right back up. Thanks anyway," Aaron said.

Meanwhile, back at the hospital, when Anita, Ebony, and Destiny reached the room that Erin and Christian were in, a physician's assistant walked over to the room door and picked up Erin's chart that was hanging on the side of the door.

"Excuse me, please," he said. "I just need to grab this chart. Oh, and good afternoon."

When he grabbed Erin's chart, he flipped through the pages and then he wrote on the papers.

Anita said to him, "Hi, I'm the patient's mother. What are you writing? Oh, first, what is your name?"

"Oh, excuse me, I'm Carl, the physician's assistant. I'm just writing Erin's progress. She's doing really well and she should make a full recovery."

"Ebony and Destiny, go on and visit with your sisters. I'll be there in a minute," Anita said.

"Carl, make sure you show on the record that Erin can possibly later develop a disorder that was caused by the blow to her head," Anita said.

"Well, I think she will make a full recovery. I don't think that will be necessary," Carl said.

Anita looked at him and said, "Right now, I don't care what you think. This is my child. I know her and you don't. The injury to her head is very serious and I want the record to show what can occur in later years. Are you currently doing your residency?"

"Yes, I am," Carl answered.

"Well, Carl, in less than one week, I will be your boss. You do as I say or you may walk out the door and don't look back. Now, you may take this to the board, on which I am the chairman of, or you can do as you are told. Do I make myself clear?" Dr. Jackson said.

"Yes ma'am (Carl put his hand over his mouth). Oh, you are Dr. Jackson. They never said that Dr. Jackson is a woman. Yes, Doctor. You made it very clear," Carl said.

"And Carl, make this a learning experience. Unless you have studied neurology, you never know how the brain will function later after a blow to the head. We always pray healing, but in case the brain becomes unstable, it will be on record that the blow to Erin's head could possibly be the cause for any erratic behavior. Are you following me?" Anita said.

"Yes ma'am, I am, and I will put it on record," Carl said.

"Thank you, Carl, now let me see how my girls are doing," Anita said.

When Anita went into the room, Erin looked at her and started to cry. Anita went over to her and said, "What's wrong? Why are you crying?"

As Anita wiped Erin's tears, Erin said, "I thank God that He did not let me lay on the floor and die. I love you and I'm happy to see you, Mommy. Where's Daddy?"

"Right now, your daddy is probably at you all's school. He said that he will be here later, and also Junior wanted me to tell you that he loves the both of you and to tell you, Erin to clock it," Anita said.

Erin was still under heavy pain medication for the open wound on her head, so she sounded groggy. "As soon as I can, I'm going to do just that," she said.

"Well, let me look at the both of you. How are you feeling?" Anita asked.

"The doctors came in a few times today to see Erin and me. They checked the stitches on my neck. They cleaned the cut and put some type of ointment on it. Then they bandaged it up really thick. You see I have this brace on. It allows me to be able to lay on my back without disturbing the stitches. I will keep the bandage on for 12 hours and off for 12 hours so that it will get air, and they said the brace will limit my neck movement. They checked my nerves and had me to move my head up and down and side to side. My head hurts, but not like it did yesterday and last night. They are giving me Ibuprofen for any pain or swelling," Christian said.

"When the doctors came to evaluate me, they wanted me to repeat everything they said. Some of it didn't make sense," Erin said.

"Mommy, she failed the test. I tried to repeat what they were saying and I couldn't get it either," Christian said.

"They also wanted me to tell them my age and my date of birth. They asked me if I knew who Chris was. They gave me math problems. They also wanted me to tell them why I was in the hospital," Erin said.

"Well, how do you think you did on your evaluation?" Anita asked.

"I think I did ok, not really good, but ok. I told the doctors that I don't remember anything about what happened. All I know is I heard a loud sound in my ears and I became very dizzy. I know that I'm in the hospital with a head injury, and as soon as I get better, I'm gonna find who did this and I am going to clock them," Erin said.

At the school, Mr. Dean came out of his office and extended his hand to Aaron.

"Mr. Jackson, I'm sorry about what happened to your daughters in this school," he said.

Mr. Dean looked at Jeff. "Haven't we met?" he said.

"We met for the first time yesterday. I'm Officer Harrison, one of the investigating officers on the scene," Jeff said.

"Oh yes, Officer Harrison," as Mr. Dean extended his hand to Jeff.

Then Mr. Dean said, "What can I do for the both of you gentlemen today?"

"Mr. Dean, if you can walk around the school with us, maybe you can tell us what you know about yesterday. And if you will, please bring a copy of Erin's and Christian's class schedules for the day of the attack," Aaron said.

"Sure, let me grab my notes off my desk. I'll be right back," said Mr. Dean.

The dean moved swiftly to his office to grab his notes. He returned and said, "Ok, gentlemen (he handed the papers to Aaron), here are the schedules of the two girls that were injured yesterday. If you're ready, we can go this way."

Aaron, Jeff, and Mr. Dean walked out of the office.

Aaron and Jeff turned on their recorders as they walked down the hallway.

"Mr. Dean, when my daughters were attacked, can you tell us around what time it was that someone reported seeing Erin lying in a puddle of blood, and who was the person that found her?" Aaron asked.

"Sure, it was around 3:45 p.m. in the afternoon. That's when Bridgett Sampson, one of our freshmen, saw your daughter lying in the hall, and she ran down to the office for help," Mr. Dean said.

"Erin," Aaron said.

"Excuse me," Mr. Dean said.

"My daughter, Erin is her name," Aaron said.

"Oh, pardon me," Mr. Dean said.

"Can you tell us about the attack on Christian?" Aaron said.

"It was April Edmonds who saw Christian walking in a daze, holding one hand on her neck leaning on the wall. She first noticed Christian was looking lethargic and then she noticed blood on her blouse. That's when she screamed and ran for help," Mr. Dean said.

"Around what time was that?" Aaron said.

"I would say it was, oh maybe, 10 to 15 minutes later," Mr. Dean said.

As they walked up the stairs to the locations of the attacks, Mr. Dean said, "When it was brought to our attention, we immediately dispatched out our hall monitoring team to see what was going on. They radioed us and told us to call for an ambulance. It was 8 minutes exactly when the paramedics arrived. My assistant, Frederick, went up with the paramedics."

"What are the protocols when an incident such as this occurs in the school?" Aaron asked.

"Well, we sound the alarm and lock all the doors," Mr. Dean said.

"In a case like this, such as a brutal attack on two students, once the doors were locked, was there any kind of in-house investigation, like asking the hall monitors to walk the floors to see if anyone was walking around without their student ID or going around from room to room asking the teachers if all the students that are in their class belong in that class?" Aaron asked.

"Well, everything happened so fast and something like this has never happened in the school. We weren't ready for this. The teachers were not notified in a timely manner and the hall monitors did not look for the attacker. We really need to polish up on our training," Mr. Dean said.

The attack on Erin was on the second floor. They were at the location where she fell, and it was close to the ladies' room door. A mop closet separated the ladies' room and the men's room.

"This is the location where Erin was found!" Jeff said.

"Oh, I didn't know it was just outside of the ladies' room," Mr. Dean said.

"What do you mean, you didn't know? You are the dean over the whole school. You mean to tell me that a student, my child, was wounded in this building, she laid here in a puddle of blood, and you never came to even see what was going on?" Aaron said.

"I am sorry, but I was in such a panic. I simply lost it. I couldn't focus or function during that time," Mr. Dean replied.

"Mr. Dean, everything is not going to be smooth sailing. When the going gets tough, you've got to learn how to roll with the punches and come out swinging," Aaron said.

"Forgive me, I don't understand!" Mr. Dean said.

"Never mind, I didn't think you would," Aaron replied.

"I see that class is in session now. Let me see, (Aaron looked on Erin's class schedule and said to himself out loud, 'Anatomy,' then he looked at Mr. Dean) is that Ms. Parsons?"

"Yes, it is," Mr. Dean said.

"Will both of you wait right here for a minute while I speak with Ms. Parsons?" Aaron asked.

"You know I will," Jeff said.

"Oh, go right ahead, take your time, sir," Mr. Dean said.

Aaron walked into Ms. Parsons's classroom and over to her desk. When she saw him approach her, she stood up and said, "How may I help you, sir?"

Then Aaron said, "Ms. Parsons, my name is Aaron Jackson. My daughter Erin was in your class yesterday when she was attacked. Do you mind stepping out in the hall to talk with me for a few minutes?"

"Oh no, sure I can. By the way, how is Erin?" Ms. Parsons asked.

"If it's ok with you, I'd like to talk in the hall," Aaron said.

Ms. Parsons quietly said, "Oh sure. Class, I will be right out in the hall, talking with a parent, if you need me."

Aaron and Ms. Parsons walked out of the classroom and into the hall. They stood over by Mr. Dean and Jeff. Aaron introduced Jeff to Ms. Parsons, and Jeff handed her one of his business cards and said, "It's nice to meet you Ms. Parsons, please call me if you can think of anything."

Then Aaron said, "Ms. Parsons, my daughter was hurt very badly yesterday and I need to know if you saw anything or heard anything during that time."

"Well, Erin is one of my best and brightest students. How is she by the way?" Ms. Parsons asked.

"Ms. Parsons, will you please answer the question?" Aaron asked.

"Oh sure, well yesterday, I didn't have my glasses when I did my roll call. I called Quentin Tellers's name and for a few seconds no one said anything, so I repeated his name again; and that's when the voice of a young man answered that was not familiar to me. It was kind of raspy. I looked up, but my vision was blurred. I do know he was wearing a yellow and blue polo type of shirt. So I said to myself, 'Maybe he has allergies.' Anyway, a few minutes after Erin came to say that she was going to the ladies' room, the young man who I thought was Quentin went out the other door and he never came back. It was maybe 15 to 20 minutes later when the alarm sounded. I noticed Erin's books were still on the desk. I could see that because she sits right in the front of the class," Ms. Parsons said.

"Ms. Parsons, is Quentin in class now?" Jeff asked.

"Yes, he is," answered Ms. Parsons.

"I'm going to need to speak with him. Also, if I can get a copy of the students that were in class yesterday, I would appreciate that," Jeff said.

"Oh sure, I can give that to you right now," Ms. Parsons said.

"Ms. Parsons, if you don't mind, while you're making the copy, if you will ask Quentin if he would come out into the hall for a brief minute." Jeff added.

"I sure will send him right out. I am more than happy to help in any way," Ms. Parsons said.

Ms. Parsons walked back into her classroom. Jeff pulled out his pad and pen. A few seconds later, Quentin came out and said, "Ms. Parsons said that I was needed in the hall. How can I help you?"

"Quentin, I'm Officer Harrison and this is Mr. Jackson. I am sure you know Mr. Dean. Quentin, yesterday, were you in Ms. Parsons's class?"

"No, I wasn't in school yesterday!" Quentin answered.

"We are asking because someone answered to your name during roll call," Jeff mentioned.

"I know, that's so weird. A couple of my classmates told me that. I had a doctor and a dental appointment yesterday," Quentin said.

"Can I get the names of the students who heard the guy answer to your name?" Jeff asked.

"Oh sure, it was Beth Winston, Lilly Oliver, and Stanley Michaels," Quentin answered.

"I thank you, Quentin, you may go back in class. Oh, and Quentin, don't mention what was said out here. If I have any more questions, I'll contact you, thank you," Jeff said.

"Ok, how are we going to handle this? We need to make sure that these four students don't talk to anyone about this, Mr. Dean. Can you go in the class and get all three of the students and bring them out together? We just have to separate each one of them while we talk with them," Jeff said.

"Sure, I'll do that right now," Mr. Dean said.

When Mr. Dean walked into the classroom, Jeff and Aaron walked several feet down the hall.

Jeff said, "We need space between the students when they come out of their class. We will call them over one at a time and have one of them to stand on the other side of the hall, keeping them both with Dean Dong. It's no telling what he may tell them."

"You're right about that," Aaron said.

So when the students came out into the hall with Mr. Dean, Jeff pointed and said, "If I can have one of you to stand on the other side of the hall, and if one of you will come over here, please."

"Oh sure, I'll come," Lilly said.

As Lilly moved swiftly in a tiptoe fashion, like walking on hot rocks, she reached Jeff and Aaron.

"Hi, Lilly, I'm Officer Harrison, and this is Mr. Jackson. Lilly, yesterday there was a person in class who answered to Quentin's name when Ms. Parsons called the roll. Did you know that person?"

Lilly giggled and said, "Oh sorry, but it was funny, that guy pretending to be Quentin and Ms. Parsons didn't know that it wasn't Quentin." When Lilly looked at Aaron and Jeff, she saw that they were not amused at all. Lilly's facial expression changed, she wiped the smile off real fast and said, "No, I didn't know him, but what I did was take a picture of him with my phone to show this guy to Quentin, but I forgot."

"Oh, you have a picture? May I see it?" Jeff asked.

"Yes, you can, but my phone is in my purse in class," Lilly answered.

"Do you mind if I stand by the classroom door while you get your phone?" Jeff asked.

"Oh, absolutely not," Lilly answered.

As Jeff and Lilly walked to the classroom, he opened the door for her and he stood outside of the door looking inside. When Lilly came back, Jeff opened the door and they walked back to where Aaron was standing.

"Let me see." As Lilly scrolled through her phone, she said, "Here he is. (She passed the phone to Jeff.) It's only a side view of the guy."

"A side view is better than no view at all!" Aaron said.

Jeff answered and then he said to Lilly, "Do you mind if I hold your phone for a minute, and can you stand over there while I make a call?"

"Oh, go right ahead," Lilly answered, as she stepped to the side. Jeff walked away and Aaron walked with him.

He showed Aaron the picture of the guy. Then Aaron said, "I'm going to need a copy of that picture. I'm not going to let my family know about this. I don't want to alarm them anymore!"

"I'm calling my office. I need to send this picture to them and have it run through the database to see if we come up with something, and then I need to delete it off this girl's phone. When I go into the office, I'll make a copy for you," Jeff said.

While Jeff was holding for someone to answer, he asked Aaron, "Does this face look familiar to you?"

"If I can remember those faces back then, this kind of looks like the boy, Billy Goldstein. He's the one who said he and his family hate blacks," Aaron said.

"I don't care what his family hates, whoever he is. When we catch him, we're going to show his white ass and his family what blacks do when they hate us for no reason. We'll see him in court," Jeff said.

"Nia, hey, this is Officer Jeff Harrison. Nia, I need to send a picture over to you. Listen, I'm at the university where the two sisters were attacked yesterday. Are you near the composite computer?" he asked.

"Yes, I am, and it is on," Nia answered.

"Ok, I'm sending this picture over to you right now. You should be getting it in a few seconds," Jeff said.

"Is it a side view of a guy wearing a yellow and blue shirt?" Nia asked.

"Yes, you got it. Please try and find out everything you can about this creep," Jeff said.

"I sure will, and when I get something, I will send it right to you. I'll get the information back to you," Nia said.

"Thanks," Jeff said.

When Jeff's call ended, he said, "Now let me delete this picture."

Aaron and Jeff walked over to Lilly. Jeff handed her the cell phone and he said, "I'm sorry, but the picture had to be deleted while we do our investigation. Lilly, please don't mention this conversation to anyone, thank you. That's all we have. You can return to class."

Then Jeff called Stanley Michaels. As Stanley walked over to talk with Jeff and Aaron, Jeff said, "How are you doing today, Stanley?"

Stanley says, "I'm ok!"

"Stanley, do you know why we called you out here today?" Jeff said.

"I think it's about what happened to Erin yesterday!" Stanley said.

"Do you know anything about that?" Jeff asked.

"No, but what I do know is that Erin didn't deserve that. I like Erin. She's a cool girl. Sometimes I have lunch with her and her sisters. I think they are all cool. Why would someone do something like that?" Stanley said.

"That's what we are trying to find out. This is Mr. Jackson, Erin's dad," Jeff said.

Stanley reached out his hand to shake Aaron's hand and said, "It's nice to meet you, Mr. Jackson, your daughters are awesome."

"Thanks, Stanley. It's nice to meet you too. Stanley, the guy in the classroom yesterday who answered to Quentin's name when the roll was called, do you know him?"

"No, but I've seen him hanging around the school a few times, in the library and in the cafeteria. He never talks to anyone, but the two other guys I've seen him with, they are kind of geeky. I do know he drives a black jeep. It was parked over by your daughters' car yesterday," Stanley mentioned.

"Did you notice anything different on the jeep that would stand out?" Jeff asked.

"I noticed the front bumper has a dent on it and the back has a skeleton skull sticker," Stanley said.

"Can you describe the other two guys?" Jeff asked.

"Both the guys are white. Both are about 6 feet tall. One has sandy blond hair and a Fu Manchu moustache. The other guy's hair is dark brown and it comes down to his shoulders. They always have on jeans and boots," Stanley added.

"Is that everything you can tell us?" Jeff asked.

"That's all I can think of right at this moment," Stanley answered.

Jeff handed Stanley his card and said, "Please call me if you think of anything else and please keep this chat to yourself."

Jeff looked at Aaron and said, "Is there anything you want to add?"

Aaron shook Stanley's hand and said, "You've been very helpful. My family and I thank you."

As Stanley, Jeff, and Aaron walked back up the hall towards Mr. Dean and Beth Winston, Stanley went back into class.

Jeff said, "Hi, Beth, I am Officer Harrison and this is Mr. Jackson. Beth, we just have a couple of questions to ask you. On yesterday, you know what happened to Erin and her sister, don't you?"

"Yes, and it was awful," Beth answered.

"Yes, I agree. There was a guy in your class that didn't belong in there. Did you know him?" Jeff asked.

"No, I don't know him, but I saw him a couple of times hanging with Richard, a guy who asked me for my number, and when I refused to give it to him, he called me a stuck up bitch!" she said.

"Do you know Richard's last name?" Jeff asked.

"He didn't give it to me; he was kind of creepy," Beth said.

"Beth, here's my card. If you have anything more about this guy Richard, please call me and please don't talk about this," Jeff said.

"Oh, I won't. How is Erin doing?" Beth asked.

"She's getting better. I haven't seen her today. I'll be heading over to the hospital when I leave the school. Thank you for asking," Aaron said.

"Oh, no problem. I like Erin. Will you tell her that I asked about her?" Beth said.

"I sure will," Aaron said.

"Let's go up to the third floor and see if Ms. Edmonds is in class," Aaron said.

As they walked up the hallway and before they went up the stairs, Aaron said, "Mr. Dean, I'm going to have to make this quick, I have to get over to the hospital." Aaron pulled out a folder from his briefcase and a sheet of paper. He wrote Peter Pitts, Richard Rivers, Billy Goldstein, and Bobby Spinks on it and he handed it to Mr. Dean. "These four names are boys who harassed my daughters when they were in elementary school, do you mind? I need to know if they are enrolled in this school. Officer Harrison has Christian's schedule, we'll be ok going alone with this one."

"Oh, I'll get right on this. I should have the information for you when you come back down into my office," Mr. Dean said.

"Thank you, sir," Aaron said. So Aaron and Jeff walked up the stairs hoping that the student who saw Christian in the hall was in class today. They first stopped by Christian's class and talked with her teacher, Mr. Chase Boone.

When Aaron and Jeff walked into Professor Boone's class, he greeted them by saying, "Gentlemen, how may I help you?"

"Professor Boone, my name is Mr. Jackson. I am Christian Jackson's father, and this is Officer Harrison," Aaron said.

"Nice to meet you both. How is Christian doing? I'm so sorry for what happened to her. How may I assist you?" Professor Boone asked.

"Well, we are trying to locate Sheena Edmonds. Is she in your class, and has anyone mentioned anything that could help us with this investigation?" Jeff asked.

"Sheena Edmonds is one of my students, but she will be in class on tomorrow, and the only talking that I've heard is the students expressing their concern and safety in the school. If I may get a card, I will give it to Sheena on tomorrow," Professor Boone said.

Jeff gave the professor his card and said, "Thank you for your time. If you have any information for us, please call me."

"I sure will. Enjoy the rest of your day," Professor Boone said.

"We're going to try," Jeff said, as they walked out the classroom door.

"Jeff, will you show me where the weapons were found, please?" Aaron said.

"Sure, AJ, right this way," he said.

They walked swiftly down the stairs and back up the hall to the men's bathroom. They went inside and Jeff pointed to the trash can.

"As you can see, we dusted everything in this room for fingerprints. We took the bag out of the can and took it to the headquarters. We are testing every paper towel; no stone will be unturned in this investigation!" Officer Harrison stated.

When they left the men's room, they headed down to Mr. Dean's office. They discussed why this tragedy happened and that the maniac was still on the loose. They both questioned if the guys were there for revenge only, and what the school was going to do about security for the students.

When Aaron and Jeff walked into the office, Lauren, the dean's clerk, said, "Mr. Dean is expecting you. You can go right into his office."

Jeff and Aaron walked into Mr. Dean's office. "Take a seat, gentlemen," he said. "I have no one enrolled in this school by any of these names!"

Aaron looked at Jeff, Jeff looked at Aaron, and Aaron said with a puzzled look, as his head leaned to one side, "I can't believe these four young guys would travel this far just to do harm to my daughters."

Aaron looked at Mr. Dean and said, "Are you sure, not one name? I had your clerk to check and she also found nothing. I wonder if any of them changed their names."

"Yes, I am sure. None of these names came up when I entered the names into the computer. If they changed their names, we won't know who they are until someone actually sees these guys. Mr. Jackson, tell me exactly what happened when your children were in elementary school that involved these four boys," Mr. Dean said.

"My daughters were bullied many times by these four guys. I had a meeting with the school's principal and we met with each of them, one-on-one. These boys had very little on their minds back then, nothing but hate for blacks. My girls were fed up with their stuff and they kicked those boys' asses. I'm going to say this, Mr. Dean. My family and I did not travel this far to be bullied once again by the same little hateful monsters, thinking that they are going to interrupt, stop, or even block them from getting their diplomas. My daughters will walk across the stage. When my daughters return back to this school, they will have security and I mean armed security. Mr. Dean, what happened yesterday will not happen again, I assure you. If blood is going to be mopped up on these floors or washed away outside, it will be the blood of one of those punks. You see, Mr. Dean, I don't play when it comes to any of my loved ones. Do I make myself clear? (Aaron hit Mr. Dean's desk with his fist.) I'm sick of this shit!" Aaron boldly explained.

Aaron then stood up and said, "Come on, Jeff. I've got to go see my babies."

So Jeff and Aaron left the school. They got into Aaron's car and headed to the hospital.

Aaron said, "Man, I'm telling you this is some bull crap. This ain't nothing but the work of the devil. God is testing my faith. I trust you, Lord, that you will reveal these jokers and remove each one of them out of my family's lives forever, in Jesus' name, Amen. You know I refuse to believe that none of them are enrolled in the school. What is going on, Jeff, man? I need to go see that little bastard that's being held without bond. On second thought, I'd better stay away because the anger I have in me, I could just walk up to him, grab his throat, and rip his Adam's apple right out!"

"Before I say anything, let me make a call." Jeff reached in his pocket, pulled out his cell phone, and made a call.

While the phone rang, Jeff said, "Aaron, man this is going to all unfold. They can run, but they can't hide for long."

While Jeff was still talking to Aaron, the person on the other end said, "Hello."

Jeff said, "Oh hey, Freda, it's Jeff-"

"I know who it is," Freda interrupted. "How are you?" she asked.

"I'm good," Jeff answered.

"Don't sound like you're good to me. When I answered the phone, I heard you say, 'They can't hide for long,'" Freda said.

"Oh, I was talking with Aaron; he's the dad of the two sisters that were hurt yesterday. Freda, the boy that's being held without bond for the assault, it's three more of them. They need to be caught," Jeff said.

"You mean the assault on the two sisters, correct?" Freda asked.

"Yes, I'm with their dad. We are on the way to the hospital. We just left the school. But listen, if you and Sam aren't busy on this Saturday, can we get together? I want you to meet him and his wife. He has a lot of information I think you would want to hear," Jeff said.

"Saturday sounds good, what, around 7ish?" Freda said.

"AJ, 7 o'clock. Is that time good for you and Nita?" Jeff asked. Aaron nodded his head.

"Freda, AJ said 7 is a good time," Jeff said.

"I am at Tampa General now. I had some work done on my foot. Is this where the girls are?" Freda asked.

"Yes, that's where we're heading to right now," Jeff answered.

"What room are they in?" Freda asked.

"AJ, what room are your daughters in?" Jeff asked.

"Room 206," Aaron answered.

"Room 206, Freda," Jeff replied.

"Well, I'll meet you there. I'll go on up and introduce myself," Freda said.

"Thanks, Freda. We will see you shortly," Jeff said.

After the phone call ended, Jeff and Aaron gave a high five and Aaron said very loudly, "Ok, little punks, we are coming after y'all's asses. I'm getting ready to meet one of Florida's heavy hitters. You know, Jeff, I had cases in Judge Perkins's court. When she sees me, I'm sure she will remember me. Come on light, change."

Aaron and Jeff arrived at the hospital. They parked the car and got out. As they walked into the hospital's doors, Jeff said, "Both Freda and Sam are cool people; but when she puts on that robe, boy it's on; she don't play. Freda believes in what's right, you'll see."

They walked into Erin and Christian's room. Christian held her arms out and said, "Daddy," just like a little girl.

Aaron went over and gave Christian a kiss on her forehead and a hug.

Then he said, "How are you feeling today, pumpkin?"

Christian said, "I'm feeling a lot better today, Daddy."

Then he kissed Destiny and Ebony. He went over to Erin. "Sugar bear, how are you feeling today?"

Erin said, "Daddy, I hurt a little. I'm still getting antibiotics and pain medication. Daddy, you know I'm going to clock them."

"Well, let's think about getting better first," Aaron said.

Then Aaron turned around and looked at Freda and said as he walked over to where she was sitting, "Judge Perkins, it's nice to shake your hand here and not on the stand. How are you?"

"I'm well. I'm ok, just watch out for the foot," Freda said.

Then Aaron said, "Everyone, but Destiny and Ebony, this is Officer Jeffery Harrison!"

Anita walked over to Jeff. As she gave him a hug, she said, "I thank you for caring and bringing my babies to the hospital yesterday."

"Oh, it was no problem. As a matter of fact, AJ and I have become friends and that's a hard thing to find. We just clicked, I'm thankful," Jeff said.

"I'm thankful as well, Jeff," Aaron said.

Jeff looked at Ebony and Destiny. He waved saying, "How are you doing?"

Both the girls said, "Hi, Officer Harrison."

Jeff looked at Freda and said, "Isn't this amazing? Look how God works. When you look at these girls, you can't tell one from the other."

"I thought the same thing when I walked into the room. They are beautiful girls. I'm sorry something like this happened," Freda said.

"Attorney Jackson, haven't I seen you in my courtroom before?" Freda asked.

"Yes, you have, Judge Perkins, many times," Aaron answered.

"Judge Perkins, in the courtroom and Attorney Jackson, but when work is over, it's no one's business what kind of relationship we share," Freda said.

Then Aaron, Freda, and Jeff sat in the chairs facing each other.

"Nita, you care to join us?" Freda said.

"Not right now. I know whatever you all discuss, it will be pillow talk tonight. If I need to add anything or if you need me, I'll be right there," Nita said.

"Ok, thanks," Freda said.

They started talking. Freda said to Aaron, "I had a good visit with your family. They enlightened me about a lot. I wrote my notes. Let me tell you what I have. I know your girls were bullied in elementary school and they gave me the names of the four guys. They saw two of them at the school, and someone blew a blow dart and hit one of your daughters on the leg. I do know that someone came up from behind and attacked two of your daughters. You know, I find this odd, but I'm not saying it's impossible. I've never had a case like this before. Something that stemmed over more than ten years ago. We have to stop these boys and put them away for good, AJ, if you don't mind me calling you that!"

"Oh no, Freda, I feel like this will be a friendship that will last a lifetime," Aaron added.

"Well today, at the school, we learned from the dean, whose name is Mr. Dean, that none of those boys are enrolled in the school. We don't know if they changed their names. We talked with some of the students that were in Erin's class yesterday and one of those boys sat in the class and answered to the roll. The professor left her glasses at home, so she couldn't recognize anyone and thought the student may have had a cold or something. But one of the students took a picture of this jerk, another student described one. So when Erin left the class to go to the bathroom, a few minutes later is when the little rat gets up and leaves the class. One of their names is Richard," Aaron said.

"Ok, we have one guy in custody and we have descriptions of two more. We know that one name is still Richard. Let's see what we come up with in the next few days. On Monday, Peter Pitts will be in my courtroom. Right now, he is being charged for destruction of personal property. I contained him because of what happened to Erin and Christian. Now his description does not fit the guy who sat in the classroom. That's who I think attacked Erin. It had to have been more than one person if the attacks happened close in time. Tomorrow, I will locate all four boys or their parents. Someone is going to be held responsible for this. They will have stay away orders issued. If they disobey, each one of those boys' parents will be ordered to pay a healthy fine. That Pitts boy or his parents are going to pay dearly on Monday. I'm going to go home. I will see you on Monday, correct, Jeff? And I will see you and Nita at Kendra Taste on Saturday," Freda said.

"Yes, you will, Freda. We thank you for stopping by. We covered a lot in a short time," Aaron said.

Freda said goodbye to everyone and she left the room.

When the meeting with Freda was over, Jeff said, "I am happy to meet both of you, Erin and Christian. One thing I don't have to worry about is putting a face with the name, and Nita, it's nice to meet the mother of such beautiful girls and that straightforward husband of yours. I'm very sorry for what you and your family are going through, but you can rest assure that me and my buddies are on the case. I hope we are the ones who catch these boys. We are really going to bring back the eighteen hundreds. The only difference is the master is black, you hear me when I say, and we are going to put a hurting on them. Who do they think they are? You got your butts kicked by girls. Keep it to yourselves and get over it. If the white officers catch them, they will be pampered. No sir, not I."

"Christian can now be discharged, but she wants to stay here with Erin until tomorrow. That's when they both will be coming home," Anita said.

"I'm sure glad we have good insurance. Who wants to stay in the hospital another day when you can go home? But I do understand, pumpkin, I know it's your sister and you don't want to leave her alone. That's another thing I need to mention to Freda is make the parents of those untrained monsters pay for the girls' hospital stay," Aaron said.

When Saturday came, they all greeted each other at Kendra Taste, along with Marques Cooke and his wife Karen, Brian Thompson and his wife Carolyn, and Tyree Bellamy with his bride Kimberly. It went well. The food was delicious. The environment put them all in a peaceful frame of mind. They exchanged numbers and they talked about family, the challenges they faced, the hurdles they had to jump over, things they regretted, traveling, and other subjects. They enjoyed each other's company so much that the restaurant closed and they were still talking.

Marques, Brian, and Tyree were also on the police force and they would be protecting Destiny, Erin, Christian, and Ebony while they were in school. Judge Freda Perkins told them that she will file papers to make sure they will be paid while on duty at the school.

After the girls were discharged from the hospital, Aaron told them, "Don't focus on what happened at school. You know that Marques,

Brian, Tyree, and Jeff will be there as long as you are in the school. I brought cell phones for each one of you (he handed the bag of cell phones to Anita). Choose your colors. We are going to make sure right now that we program every number that we need, so y'all call each other, and put your grandparents' numbers, your aunts, uncles, cousins, and friends in it. I'm going to write down the security guys' names and numbers along with Jeff's. If anything happens, make sure you get somebody on the line. Tell them everything you can. Is that understood?"

While in court with Judge Freda Perkins, Peter's parents tried to cover for him, but the court was not accepting it. Judge Freda wanted to know if they knew Billy Goldstein, Richard Rivers, and Bobby Spinks. Peter's parents said they did know the boys. The judge ordered his parents to serve the stay away orders to each one of those boys' parents and send the signed copies back to her office within 48 hours.

Judge Perkins told Peter's parents that what the boys are doing will cause them a lot of time in jail and if she sees them in her courtroom again, they will be punished to the full extent, and the Jacksons will be entitled to a very big lawsuit.

Monday afternoon, while at work, Jeff called and said, "Hey, AJ. Did Freda call you?"

"No, not yet. I saw her briefly, but she didn't see me. I had court all day!" Aaron said.

"Well, she called me and the little punk is out. They let the bastard go. He has a stay away order against all of them. He's on six months' probation. He has to pay you guys $1,500 for damages and do six months of community service. Freda was able to contact every last one of those guys' parents and she laid it on them. Now it's up to them to control their litter or they are going to pay," Jeff said.

"As long as they keep their funky tails away from me and my family, we are alright. Look, Jeff, I have to be in court in five minutes. We'll talk later," Aaron said.

"Ok cool, later man," Jeff replied.

It took a few weeks before Erin started feeling like herself again. While she was at home recuperating, she watched her favorite martial artist, Steven Segal. She would practice the moves that he did. She also liked the tactics that Charles Bronson used; she could watch them all day long.

Christian healed quicker, but her wound still hurt in spots.

They were all back to doing what they loved, their daily workouts, running, flipping, kicking, just having fun together, and staying fit.

Before the girls went back to school, Nita and Jeff went to make sure that the stay away orders on all four guys were still in place. Aaron told the judge that they were not students at the school. Judge Freda Perkins advised each one of their parents that they will be held accountable for any wrongdoing while under this order.

The orders were granted.

Going back to school went smoothly for all of the girls. They drove their car and when they arrived, their security team was waiting on the steps of the school. They got the schedules of each sister. The plan that the officers put in place went really well.

There was one month until the girls graduate and they were all excited. They've discussed what they wanted in their future and have even dreamt dreams about it. As they got closer to graduation, they were excited and realized that they were closer to all of the plans they discussed coming true. Lots of family and old friends were going to travel to Florida to give their congrats to the quads.

On the wall, in the family room, Anita hung pictures of each one of her children in their cap and gown. She had them blown up to 16" x 32" in size, with Aaron Jr. in the middle and his four sisters around him.

When she was done, she stood back and said, "Aaron, honey, come see this."

Aaron came into the room and said, "I like it. Look at all of our beautiful children."

"Yep, four and one," Anita said.

After dinner, the girls went into the kitchen to clean it up. Once they were done, Destiny yelled from the kitchen, "Mom and Dad, we're going for a run. We won't be gone long!"

"Des, come in here," Anita yelled back.

"Mommy, now I know that you could hear every word I said, didn't you?" Des said.

"Yes, your dad and I both heard every word. Where are you all going jogging at?" Anita asked.

"I guess around in the neighborhood or maybe around on the elementary school track. We all have our cell phones with us. We know both you and Daddy love us and you are concerned about us. But just keep in mind that we are God's children and we are all here for a season, so when it's our time, it's our time. You see, God was not ready for Chris or Erin, and they are fine. Don't worry, we'll be ok. Now stand so I can give you and Daddy a big kiss and a hug," Destiny said.

Both Anita and Aaron stood up while Des gave both of them a hug and a kiss. "I love you Mommy and I love you Daddy," she said.

"We love you too, pumpkin, now be safe," they responded.

"We will," Des responded.

So the girls left out the door. They started doing some stretches as they talked and then they got their run on. The girls headed down to the elementary school which was about a mile and a half away.

When they reached the school grounds, they started walking around the tracks. The lighting was really bright and they felt safe. As the girls walked and talked, they saw other shadows on the ground, so they stopped and turned around. When they did, they were in shock. It was Peter Pitts, Richard Rivers, Billy Goldstein, and Bobby Spinks. All four of the guys made a circle around the girls. Erin, Christian, Destiny, and Ebony looked at the guys, then they looked at each other.

The girls went into their karate stance, and Erin said, "Clock it." Each sister took a man. They fought those guys; and when they kicked them to the ground, Erin yelled, "Run."

They ran off the school grounds and up the street. They all tried to reach for their cell phones, while running as fast as they could, even though they were exhausted from the fight.

Erin asked, "Are we all together?"

Ebony said, "Yes."

Christian said, "Yes."

And then Destiny said, "Yes."

And so they kept on running. They looked back and saw headlights coming up really fast. Destiny reached Anita on the phone, in hysterics, she yelled, "Mom, they are after us!"

In a panicked voice, Anita said, "Who's after you?"

As Anita pushed the record button on her phone, she heard Destiny say, "Richard Rivers, Peter Pitts, Bobby Spinks, and Billy Goldstein!"

"Where are you?" Anita asked.

"Running home," Destiny answered.

Then Erin said, "Are we all together?"

Destiny said "Yes."

Ebony said, "Yes."

Christian said, "Yes."

"Stay on the phone with me. Aaron is on the way," Anita said.

As the jeep got closer on the sisters, Destiny said, "Mom, they are coming up behind us; they are driving!"

"What are they driving?" Anita asked.

Right as Destiny turned to look back, the jeep was right up on her. She yelled, "A black jeep."

They tapped her with the truck. She dropped her phone and she fell down.

Anita yelled out Destiny's name over and over but no response.

Erin yelled again, "Are we all together?"

Christian yelled, "Yes."

Ebony yelled, "Yes."

And when Destiny didn't answer, they stopped running and turned around. The distance between them and where Destiny fell was too far away. As they yelled out Destiny's name, they could see headlights and the guys putting her into a vehicle, so they started running back towards the vehicle. The person driving the jeep made a U-turn and drove away very fast.

When Destiny called Anita's phone, Aaron started tracking Destiny's phone. Just as Aaron drove up the street, he saw three of his girls.

"Oh God, no. Father, I need thee right now, Lord. One of my children is not accounted for. I ask you, God, to please protect her, Father. Please give me and my family the strength that we need right now, in Jesus' name I pray, Amen," he said.

Aaron reached the girls. They were crying and out of control. He got out of the truck and Ebony yelled, "They got Des, Dad. They took Destiny!"

Aaron called 911. He told the dispatcher what happened, the type and color of the jeep that the boys were driving, and the location. Marques, Tyree, Jeff, and Brian heard the alert go out over the radio and they responded quickly.

The four officers started calling Aaron's phone, but Aaron could not answer their call because he was using his cell phone to track Destiny's phone. The tracking device only led him to Destiny's phone. It was laying down on the ground. He bent down and picked it up. He shook his head and answered Jeff, who was calling again.

Aaron said, "Jeff man, I saw your call. I couldn't get to you because I was tracking Destiny's phone. I just picked it up off the ground, hoping the phone would lead me to where those punks took my baby!"

"Hey look, AJ, try to stay focused. We are all over this. Why don't you go back home with Nita and I'll call you as soon as we find something?" Jeff said.

"Yeah, I need to get back home. Come on, girls. Get in the car. Your mom needs us right now. Ok, Jeff. I'll wait on the call," Aaron said.

Aaron made a U-turn. As he headed home, they all rode in silence. The radio was off and no one said a word.

When they got home, Anita ran out the house in tears. That led to all of the girls crying and talking at the same time.

Aaron said, "Let's go in the house. Someone might call us on the house phone!"

"Why don't you girls go up and take a shower? You are wet. Get those clothes off of you. Dad and I are going to put our pajamas on as well. You can come into our room when you get comfortable. All we can do now is pray," Anita said.

As soon as they all started walking up the stairs, the phone rang.

Anita said, "One of y'all run catch the phone!"

Aaron said, as he ran up the stairs, "I'm sure they are too tired to run. I'll get it."

Aaron answered the phone and it was Leslie, his mom.

"How's my oldest son doing?" she said.

With a sad, low sounding voice, Aaron's response was "Mom, I don't know!"

"Ok, that sound is not good. What's wrong, son?" Leslie asked.

"Mom, the girls went out for a jog and they took Des!" Aaron said.

In hysterics, Les said, "Oh Lord, they, who are they?"

When Aaron started to cry, his mom said, "Baby, talk to me. We are going to pray about this." Leslie's voice got louder, "Who are they, baby?"

"Those same little punks that harassed and bullied the girls when they were in elementary school!" Aaron said.

"Elementary school, elementary school! Come on, son. We got to take this to the Master," Leslie said. Then she prayed, "Father God, maker of all good things. Because you're a good God, an awesome God, Lord, we need you right now. My grandbaby Destiny is missing, Lord. You know all about this. Father, I know that you have the last say over our lives. I ask that you prepare us. Send your angels down. God, cover Destiny. Cover us with your precious blood right now, Lord. It's you and only you who can and will see us through this, I ask in Jesus' name. Whoever took my grandbaby, if any harm is afflicted upon her and her days here on earth are over, I ask that you take her up, give her a crown, and her heavenly home. In Jesus' name I do pray, Amen."

"Thanks, Mom. I'm so hurt right now. I know that my baby is gone. God prepared us before Des and the girls went jogging. She told Anita and me that she loves us and that they were God's children. She also said, 'When it's our time, it's our time.' She said that, Mom. No parent wants their child to be buried before them. Mom, I need to keep the line open. I'll call you back. I love you, Mama!" Aaron said.

"Kiss Nita and the girls for me. Tell them I love them, talk with you later," Les said.

Before Aaron could take his hand off the phone, it rang again. He picked it up quickly. He heard, "Saying hello," on the other end.

"Dad, it's me, Junior. What happened, Dad?"

"The girls went jogging, those boys chased them, and they got Des," Aaron answered.

"I'm on my way. I'll be leaving in the morning!" Junior said.

"No, it's nothing you can do but pray. You will be home for your sisters' graduation. You have less than a week or so. We will see you when it's time," Aaron said.

"How are Mom, Ebony, Chris, and Erin doing?" Junior asked.

"We are just waiting and praying!" Aaron said.

The doorbell rang and Aaron said, "Junior, talk with your mom or one of your sisters; someone's at the door. Let me go and see who it is."

"Ok, let me talk with Erin," Junior said.

"Erin, come to the phone. Junior wants to speak with you," Aaron yelled.

Erin came to the phone, while Aaron ran to the door.

Erin answered the phone and said, "Hey, brother!"

"Hi, to you, sister. How are you holding up?" Aaron Jr. asked.

"I hate that we ran so fast, not knowing that Des was so far behind us. She was talking to Mommy on the phone when they snatched her. Ebony, Chris, and I ran back, hoping that we could catch them, but they made a U-turn. We didn't know that she was so far behind," Erin explained.

"So, what happened?" Junior asked.

"Well, Des, Chris, Ebony, and I went jogging down to the elementary school. We started walking around the track talking about graduation and our future, when we saw shadows. Those four guys made a circle around us. We went into our stance. We looked them over and I yelled, 'Clock it.' Brother, we fought what seemed like forever until we got them to the ground. While they were down, we ran. And every so often, I would ask if we were all together and everyone answered. The third time I asked, Ebony and Chris were the only ones to answer. When we didn't hear Des, we stopped and looked back. We could see them putting her in the truck. We yelled out Des's name, but it was nothing we could do but run back as fast as we could. Brother, what are we going to do?" Erin said.

"All we can do is hope for the best, but prepare for the worst. Des knows how much we love her. I want to come home now, but Dad said because I have less than one week before I am due to come home, I need to wait till then," Aaron Jr. said.

"Brother, I'm going to see what's going on. But you know when I see those boys, I am going to clock them and I mean real good," Erin said.

"Oh, you don't have to tell me. I know how you are. Before we hang up, tell Mom, I love her. Tell her to keep trusting in God; He will never fail. Tell Chris and Ebony to hang in there. Look, I love you guys. I'll call you tomorrow," Junior said.

"Love you too, brother. Bye," Erin said.

Erin ran down to the door, only to see a news reporter outside setting up to report what happened, as they started rolling the camera.

The reporter started talking saying, "An AMBER alert went out just a little over an hour ago. Destiny Jackson was abducted by four white men, as her three sisters watched helplessly. I am standing at the home of Destiny, with her parents, Aaron and Anita, and her sisters. Mr. Jackson, how do you feel about this?"

"Ma'am, my family and I are heartbroken. We never understood why these boys have been after my children since elementary school. I pray that my child is ok and they will let her go. But if she is harmed in any way and I have to bury my child, hell has their names," Aaron said.

"Let's hear from Anita. (The reporter looked at Anita and could see that Anita was out of it.) The mother of Destiny Jackson is too distraught and I can understand why. Let me see if I can get one of her sisters."

The reporter went over to Christian and said, "Can you tell us what happened?"

"My sisters and I went jogging and when we saw Peter Pitts, Richard Rivers, Billy Goldstein, and Bobby Spinks at the playground, we ran. Destiny called Mommy on the phone. While she was talking to Mommy, that's when they took her," Chris said.

"Let me hear from one of the other sisters," the reporter said. So she walked over to Erin. Erin had an evil look on her face. "How are you feeling right now?" she asked Erin.

"Ma'am, you really don't want to know. I love my sister and she did not deserve what's happening to her right now. She's so kind, and I'm not so kind. She loves everyone, and I love my family, friends, and others. Destiny treated everyone with respect, and I give respect when it's given to me. They broke the chain and they will pay for what they did," Erin said.

"Reporting live outside of the home of Destiny Jackson, I am Wanda Curtis, with APX news, back to you in the station."

After the cameras stopped rolling on the Jacksons, the reporter said to the family, "Mr. and Mrs. Jackson, I am sorry for what's happening right now. I hope it all turns out with a happy ending. This must be a very stressful time for all of you just having two of your children attacked at school. Those boys will be caught. Try to have a good night."

After the reporter left the Jackson's home, the family went back inside. Walking around the house in silence, Aaron said, "Ok, it's now 1:45 in the morning. We are too quiet. We are all thinking too hard. We love Des, and if we knew where she is, we all would be going to get her right now. God knows how we feel right now. I know that none of us want to think the worst, but we have to accept what we can't change. If they took her life, I pray that someone will find my child before her body decomposes, so we can give her the proper burial that she deserves. I know without a doubt that the police are looking for her. Let's watch a funny movie. We need to laugh and not cry at this time."

Just as Aaron stopped talking, the doorbell rang and Anita said, "Oh God!"

The whole family walked to the door and it was Jeff, Marques, Brian, and Tyree. They all walked into the house in silence. Jeff said, "AJ, you know why we're here. I'm lost for words."

And then Anita said, "Jeff, is my baby gone?"

Jeff looked down shaking his head and then he looked up at Nita and said, "Yes, yes she is!"

Anita screamed out loudly, "Oh God, no. Where is she?"

Aaron, with a trembling sound in his voice said, "Jeff, they killed my baby. Those punks killed my baby. How Jeff, how?"

Erin, Christian, and Ebony hugged each other. As they cried, Chris said, "Destiny is gone, my sister is gone. Is this a dream? I can't believe my sister was murdered, taken right in front of us. Oh God, help us."

Then Jeff said, "It's best to tell you now. Let us all sit down and tell you what we know!"

So they all walked into the family room to take a seat. While the officers stood, Marques said, "AJ, Nita, Erin, Ebony, and Chris, I am so sorry for what happened. As soon as the AMBER alert went out over the radio, we were on it. You all have our numbers. Use it and don't hesitate. We are all here for you."

Aaron said, "I know that each one of you are like my brothers, thanks."

Then Brian said, "Destiny is not my blood, but when we protected the girls, she would always make us laugh. She would say, 'My uncle officers are working for that extra money and doing a good job at it. Look, you got your bulletproof vest on and y'all are walking with your shoulders stuck out.' She respected us so much to call us uncle, not only Des, but each one of the girls. It was always Uncle Tyree or Uncle Marques. She said, 'To protect someone, you have to show love for them.' Each one of the girls knew that their uncles meant business and we still do. We are always here for you, and we love you!"

"We love you, too," each one of the Jacksons said.

Then Tyree said, "You know the love that we have for you. Destiny is with the Lord now and we have to stay focused because this is a murder investigation. People are going to come to you asking questions. Don't tell them anything (and then he looked at Erin and pointed to her), especially you, niece. You know how some whites look at blacks in this world. They think they know it all and that they are right about everything. We are going to show them, in time, what we all feel right now. It will all get better!"

Jeff said, "So you leave the hard part for us. Wow, let me see how I can say it. Lord, I need your help." Then he began to sing, "*I Need Thee Every Hour.*"

With a heavy sigh, Jeff said, "Around 12:45, Destiny's body was found in that wooded area around the school. Her clothes were ripped off her. It appeared like her neck was broken. All of us stayed on the scene while the investigation was going on. They collected any evidence they could. We waited for the coroner to come get her and take her to the morgue. We told him to make sure that they do a complete autopsy on her. We knew that's what you would want. We have to take you to identify her body. We are not going to rush you. We are going to sit down, and when you are ready, we can all go together. We went by the station and got the trainers 15 passenger van."

So Aaron looked at Anita and then he looked at the girls and said, "Are we ready for this?"

"No, but we have to get ready. God is going to do what He said He will do. When we fall, He will pick us up. When we are weak, He will give us strength. And when we feel like we just can't go on, He will carry us. So we are going to let go and let God. Right now, we are not going to focus on how my baby died, but how she lived. So come on, let's put on something so we can identify Des," Anita said.

They all got up and headed up the stairs to change into something fitting for going outside.

When they came downstairs and were ready to go, Anita said, "Lord, give me strength."

Then Brian said, "Don't worry, He will."

So they left the house to go view the body. Jeff wanted to know if everyone was strong enough to go in to see Destiny's body. They all said, "Yes."

Once they arrived and went in, Aaron wanted to know if the medical examiner was a black or white person.

"I need whoever is going to do the autopsy on Destiny to be honest and not hide or cover up anything," Aaron said. "It's important to me and my family to know just how cruel and evil these demons are."

"You don't have to worry about anything. We know how the system is, but we are not going to let that happen. We made sure that Thurman, who is very thorough, takes this case. You'll meet him," Jeff said.

So they all went into the building and Jeff said, "Take a seat, wait here, and let me tell Thurman that you are here to identify the body. The other officers and I have done this numerous times. Each examiner is different, some show compassion, and some don't. Any questions that you have, ask. If you need time, you got it. I'll be back."

Jeff went in the back. He and Thurman came out wearing scrubs. Their heads and feet were covered. Aaron stood up, as Thurman walked over to him. He extended his hand and said, "Mr. Jackson, I am sorry for your loss. My name is Thurman Henson. I'll be the examiner doing the autopsy on Destiny. I have to let you and the family know that because this is a murder investigation, before you call the funeral home to come pick up the body or make any funeral arrangements, you need to be aware that the body will be here for a few weeks until every test that's being done are complete, meaning blood, tissue, sperm semen, hair, any fibers, all of that has to be returned from the lab and in my hands. Any reports and paperwork have to be completed before the body can be released!"

"Thank you, Mr. Henson," Aaron said.

"Call me Thurman. I've been dealing with these officers for a long time and they are good people. We hang out sometimes and they told me about you. Here's my card. Call anytime."

"Thanks, I will, Thurman. Let me introduce you to my family. This is my wife Anita and (as he introduced the girls, he gave an open hand gesture) my daughters, Erin, Christian, and Ebony," Aaron said.

Each girl waved their hand and said, "Hi."

Then Aaron said, "Before we go in, do you mind if we ask you a few questions?"

"Oh no, go right ahead, I am here for you!" Thurman said.

"Thurman, did my baby suffer before she died?" Anita asked.

"Anita, I can't say that she did because she just arrived about 90 minutes ago. I haven't had much time to investigate the body. But I can say that it appears to me that her neck was broken. I do know that she has blood under her fingernails, which leads me to believe that she fought her attacker or attackers. What I do first is take pictures of the body, any bruises, cuts, scratches, and anything abnormal on the body," Thurman said.

"Thurman, once you have completed everything, where do the samples go?" Aaron asked.

"We send them to a lab in California. Depending on how busy they are, it can sometimes take up to two months before we get the results. But any test that we can run here, we do," Thurman answered.

"How does my sister look?" Erin asked.

"Not bad, a little dirty, but that's because she was on the ground and we can't wash off any evidence. She has a couple of bruises, her knuckles are scarred, and she has defensive wounds," Thurman explained.

"Can we see her?" Aaron asked, and then he looked at everyone and said, "Are you all ready?"

"Yes," Anita answered.

"I'm ready, Ebony answered.

"So am I," Christian answered.

"I guess, I am," Erin said.

"What do you mean, you guess? You are ready," Aaron said.

"I said I guess because it keeps going through my head when those guys put her in that truck. If I could have only gotten to them, I would have ripped them apart, and my sister would be here right now!" Erin stated.

"Sweetie, I know that you are angry. Just let the police handle this. They know who did this and they will catch them," Anita said.

"Ok, I'm ready," Erin said.

"You know that we are here for you and we will be standing right by each one of your side," Marques said.

Then as Jeff, Brian, Tyree, and Marques stood to the side, Jeff whispered and said, "Those boys better hope we get to them before Erin does. She's going to rip them apart."

"I know it; I can see it in her; she is pissed off," Tyree said.

"If I'm around and see it happen, I'm going to let her do her thing, for real," Brian said.

"Me too, and that's no lie. They can yell for help and I won't hear nothing," Jeff said.

"That's right," Marques responded.

"Ok, let's go on back," Thurman said.

So they all headed to the back. As they walked down the hall, Thurman said, "If you will go into this room, I will roll the body over to the glass!"

"We can't touch her?" Erin asked.

"Not right now, we can't have anything to interfere with the samples that I have to collect. I know what you are going through. Once I have completed everything, I will call you, Aaron. If any of you want to stop by, feel free to do so. Just wait in this room for a few minutes," Thurman said.

As they stood waiting in the viewing room, Thurman pushed the slab with Destiny's body on it towards the viewing window. She was covered with a white sheet. As the body got closer, Anita started to tremble and the sisters started to cry. Aaron held Anita, as she turned and looked at their police friends. "I'm ok. Angels are all around us and His heavenly angels are watching over all of us right now," she said.

Destiny's body was at the window. There was an intercom that allowed you to talk to the person on the other side of the glass. Thurman pushed the button and said, "Are you all ok?"

They shook their heads yes. Then, Aaron pushed the button and said, "Can you turn the bed around so that I can see the other side of my baby's face?"

"Sure, I will," Thurman answered.

Thurman turned the slab around. Anita said, "She's at peace."

"Yes, she is," Aaron answered.

Aaron said, "Thurman, we thank you for your time. I'm sure I'll be calling you. We're going to go on home now. We have a lot of calls to make."

"No problem. Just remember Destiny is with God now. It is going to get better. Right now, it is hard to accept. Keep praying for strength. He will see you through this. I'll be looking forward to hearing from you. Try and get some rest," Thurman said.

"We will. Good night! Or should I say, 'Good morning?'" Aaron said.

As the family walked out of the viewing room, all the officers waved their hands at Thurman. Jeff said, "Thanks man," and Thurman waved back.

So the ride back home was in silence. Then Aaron said, "You know, God spoke to me and told me that all four of you are going to receive a big blessing. I'm saying this to you, Jeff, Marques, Tyree, and Brian, because all of you have been by me and my family's side, and we thank you from our hearts."

The Jacksons arrived back home. They got out of the van and Jeff said, "I'll call you all tomorrow."

"Ok, y'all be safe out there," Aaron said.

When they walked into the house, Aaron said, "I am mentally exhausted. I'm going to go upstairs and lay down. All of you can join me. We have a lot to do in the morning, lots of calls to make. Good night."

The next morning, the family got up and saw that Erin was the only one who was not upstairs. When they all came down the stairs, Anita went into the kitchen and she saw Erin out in the backyard working out. The rest of the family came into the kitchen.

Christian looked out the window and also saw Erin working out. She said, "I am still tired from yesterday. I am not going out there (and then Chris looked at Ebony). Where does she get all that energy from?"

"I don't know, but she can go right ahead. We'll call her in when breakfast is ready," Ebony answered.

The phone rang and Anita answered. "It's Henri," the voice on the other line said.

Anita said, "Hello."

Henri said, "Lord, child, how are you doing? Les called me last night."

"Mama, we are doing as best as we can right now. It's hard," she said.

Anita started to cry. Chris went over to Anita and said, "Mommy, it's going to be ok. You want me to talk to Grandma?"

Anita said, "No, I'm ok, I can talk. I just miss my child!"

When Nita got herself together, she said, "Sorry, Mama, I've been thinking about my baby, and when I do, sometimes it makes me cry!"

"Oh, you don't have to say sorry to me. I am your mother. I hate you are going through this without the rest of the family being with you," Henri said.

"You know what, Mama? We are doing better than I would expect. I know without a doubt that it's nothing but God, and I thank Him," Nita said.

"Come on now, you know it. Nothing, but the Lord. We got to give Him all the glory and the praise. How are the girls doing?" Henri asked.

"They seem to be holding up ok, Mama. Will you and Mama Les make calls to the family and friends?" Nita asked.

"Girl, you know how we do. When Les called and talked with Aaron last night, we called around and asked for prayers then," Henri said.

"Well, we went to identify the body around 4:00 this morning. It was late. They are going to do an autopsy and it may take a while. So no arrangements will be made until they can release the body to the funeral home, if anyone asks," Nita said.

"I sure hope they catch those little suckers," Henri said.

"They will; they sure will," Nita said.

"I talked with Junior. He said that he will be home for good in a few days. He is so hurt. You know that child loves his sisters," Henri said.

"I know he does. They'll be happy to see him," Nita said.

"Hey, Mama. Can I get back with you? I am getting breakfast prepared. Let me talk with you later," Nita said.

"Ok, baby. I love you, and I'll talk with you later," Henri said.

"I love you too, Mama. Ok, bye," Nita said, as she hung up the phone.

When Ebony and Chris looked out the window and saw Erin flipping, jumping, bending, just working out really hard, Ebony said, "Daddy should go tell Erin to come inside."

"Why? She's relieving tension and stress. Let her do her thing. She's upset right now because she can't get her hands on those boys. It's over for them. I wish I can get my hands on them. You know how your sister feels about y'all. She was your mother at two years old," Aaron said.

"Now that's funny," Anita laughed. "She sure did act like she was the mother over all the girls, always wanting to be the boss, but Junior was not having it. What is that he would always say to Erin? Clock it. He would have clocked her if she got out of line with him."

"So, what are we having for breakfast?" Aaron asked.

"Grits, eggs, bacon, sausage, and biscuits. I really do miss my baby, but I can't let it get me down. I am so thankful to have Des as long as we did, but thank God we still have our other children," Anita said.

"Yes, we both are, and if you need me to help you with the cooking, just let me know. We are still a team," Aaron said.

"I know we are and have been since childhood," Anita said.

"Will one of y'all ask Erin if she wants some water? I know she got to be thirsty by now," Aaron said.

So Ebony went outside and carried a glass of water to Erin and told her, "Mommy is cooking breakfast. Why don't you come in for a while?"

"I'll be in when the food is ready. Just let me know," Erin said.

Ebony went back into the house and said, "Erin said she will be in when Mommy finishes cooking."

When breakfast was ready, they called Erin in and they all ate together. They talked about graduation, the funeral, and applying for jobs. They talked about things that would make them laugh.

When they finished eating, the girls started cleaning the kitchen, and Ebony said, "Destiny really didn't like doing the dishes, so she said, 'Lord take me so that I won't have to clean the kitchen again!'"

They all laughed about that. They all knew how Destiny hated cleaning the kitchen, so Anita and Aaron both pitched in and helped.

The phone rang, Aaron answered, "Hello."

"Hey, man. It's Jeff. How are you and the family holding up?"

"Man, we are holding our own. We are thinking about all the happy times. We just finished eating breakfast and we're all pitching in cleaning the kitchen," Aaron said.

"Well, holla at me later. Tell everyone to hang in there," Jeff said.

"Oh, they will. We've got a lot of good people around us," Aaron said.

"And you know it. We are family. We ain't going nowhere," Jeff said.

So throughout the day, the family spent quality time together. They made calls to let others know what happened. To fill the empty void, everything they did, they did it together. If something was needed at the store, they all went.

While they were at the store shopping for extra food to have when Junior comes home, people would approach them. They noticed that Erin seemed to be in another world. If Erin had to say anything out of her mouth, it was defensive, so they had to shop quickly and get her home.

While driving to and from the store, Erin's eyes were like a hawk's, looking from side to side. Aaron saw how she was acting through the rearview mirror.

Before they got home, Jeff called Aaron's cell phone.

"Hey look, that reporter, Wanda Curtis, the one at the house last night. She made a comment on Erin saying that she thinks if Erin could, she would take those boys out herself. You and I know that she would, but if this gets out to the white ears, they may try to tap your phone at home or put one of those listening devices on the window to hear what is going on inside, so be cool," Jeff said.

"Thanks man, for the information," Aaron said.

When the family arrived home with the groceries, they put everything away and Erin said, "Yes! My brother will be home in four days, I am so happy!"

"We will be happy to have Junior home. It has been a long time and now we can spend time catching up on a lot that has happened while he was away. I can't wait to see pictures of the different countries he was stationed in. Once he arrives in the states, he will have to stay on base a few days," Anita said.

Aaron Jr. arrived home just two weeks before his sisters' graduation. He was very excited about starting the next phase of his life and being with his family.

Even though they couldn't see him, they talked on the phone. The closeness they shared was like none other. The tears that fell from their eyes made you think that they would never stop crying. They laughed and talked about old times over the phone.

That night, while watching a movie, Anita and Aaron started discussing

Erin. They were always on one accord; so during their discussion, Erin's behavior came up. They noticed how she shut down and stayed to herself. She became very quiet and they knew that she was thinking, plotting, and planning.

So Aaron said to Anita, "I'm going to check on Erin. See if I can bring her around before she goes off the deep end. You know how she can be revengeful."

Anita said, "Oh, you think I don't? That's my riot child. I know she can explode."

Aaron went up the stairs and he knocked on Erin's door.

"Come in," she said.

As Aaron opened the door and walked into the room, he started to sign, "Destiny's murder is an ongoing investigation and our home and phones could be tapped, so we will have to sign when certain things are being said." Erin responded back in sign, "Ok."

Aaron told Erin, "I noticed you have been working out a lot. You have been running miles and you have been practicing your karate and carrying around your numb chucks. What's on your mind, baby girl?"

Erin walked towards Aaron and began to cry out loud. He hugged her and he started to cry with her. There was no signing going on at that time.

After Erin calmed down, she said, "Daddy, I'm going to clock them. I am going to get each one of them."

Then Aaron said, "Listen, baby girl, we're going to let the law handle this. We won't forget Destiny. We will always hold the love we have for her in our hearts. I know she did not deserve what happened to her, but some people are cruel and evil. She's now resting in the arms of God and watching over all of us."

Then Erin said, "I know. You are right, Daddy."

After Aaron started to sign again, he said to Erin, "I know you, just like I know each one of my children, and you have something up your sleeve. Now, I am not trying to bury another one of my children. I know this is not normal times but normally you are the loudest, the most outgoing one in the quads. Don't have the police come knocking on my door telling me they found another one of my girls laying in a swamp somewhere. Your mother and I can't take another tragedy. Don't you understand we are hurting, too?"

Erin's response was, "Dad, there was a link taken out of the chain. We were tight like glue. We did everything together. We shared our thoughts, our dreams. I hurt so deep inside when they raped Destiny. I know she tried to fight them, so they broke her neck. She had bruises on her and we don't know what else until the autopsy comes back. Dad, do you know Ebony, Christian, and I felt her pain? Why? Because we grew together in the same womb for nine months. That's not right, she was my sister. Dad, I'm not going to tell you what I'm going to do, but if you say you know me, then you know those four white boys will pay for what they did to Destiny. I just want each one of them to feel what she felt, what we felt. It's going to be ok. My sister will rest in peace. Don't worry, Dad, I love you. I'm ok, but this is what I have to do, so don't worry. Our family will not revisit the pain of sitting through a trial that could take months, looking at all those heartbreaking pictures of Destiny's body. No, there will not be a trial. We know where Destiny's final resting place will be, but those boys, oooh no. Never will they look at any one of us with their smirk grins, saying to themselves, 'I got one of them and I am satisfied.' Well, I'm not satisfied. Not yet, Dad, I've got work to do!"

And then Erin put her hands on both sides of her dad's face and brought his head down as she kissed him on the forehead. He turned around and walked out the door.

By the time Aaron left Erin's room, Anita was upstairs and getting ready for bed.

While lying in the bed, Anita and Aaron had a conversation by signing. Aaron said, "I talked with Erin. She is hurt and heartbroken, but she said to me, 'Dad, don't worry. It will be ok.' She also said, 'If we know our child like we think we do, then those guys are in for a world of trouble.'"

Then Anita said, "I don't want our child out there fighting those crazy boys. What if they team up and hurt her? I can't stand going through another heartache."

"I know, honey; but all we can do is pray. Pray that our child will change her mind and the hate that she has built up in her will change. But, I don't think it will, so we just have to pray that God will keep her covered. If she seeks, she will find. And when she finds those boys, we have to pray that she has her sword, shield, and has on her whole armor. She is out for revenge for what they did to Chris and her. This mess probably goes back to elementary school. Who knows? We just have to pray," Aaron said.

"Well, I'm going to do just that, pray and then I'm going to sleep. Good night." Anita kissed Aaron, then she rolled over.

Later, after everyone was asleep, Erin got up out of bed. She put on her black sweats, top and bottom. She put on her running shoes, then she grabbed her numb chucks, machete, binoculars, black leather gloves, brass knuckles, duct tape, and rope. And then she grabbed a box. Inside appeared to be a flexible, five-fingered, battery-operated straw that loaded what looked like pins or nails on the end of it. When Erin took this gadget out of the box, she wanted to make sure that it was working, so she turned it on and blew into it. Those pins shot across the room and stuck into her bedroom wall. She put all of her stuff into her carrying case that had separate compartments to it and had one strap that went across the shoulder. She grabbed her flashlight that had lots of voltage, and she said, "Y'all's asses is mine!"

Erin tiptoed down the stairs and out the door she went. She got into the family's black pickup truck. She covered the bed of the truck with plastic and an old blanket.

First, Erin drove down by one of the swampy areas. She got out of the truck and started walking the distance that she would have to drag or pull the bodies. The distance of that location was not what she was looking for. Then, she shined the light just to the right of where she was standing and noticed that it was all flat, but the ground had an incline, a lot higher than where she stood. Erin saw that the trees had space between them, which led her to believe that there was a path that she could drive through, so she got back into the truck and drove to that spot, and to her surprise, the path was wide enough for her to make a U-turn.

As Erin drove slowly through the path that had a concrete ground, she made a U-turn and started backing towards the edge which had caution reflectors. She stopped the truck and got out with her flashlight in her hand. She shined the light to the left, front, and right, then she pointed it downward. She could clearly see lots of alligators and snakes in the swampy water. Erin said to herself, "Yes, this will be your final resting place, you bastards!"

Erin got back in the truck and started driving slowly up one block and down the other. She turned the radio off because she wanted to hear any loud sounding, obnoxious voices. As she continued to drive, she began thinking where could those sons of b's be and then she said, "I wonder if they are dumb enough to go back where they killed my sister. Well, we will see. Let me be smart enough to ride down to the school." As Erin got closer to the school, it started to rain really hard. Looking out at a distance, Erin could see people on the school's track field. So she thought to herself, "Let me get a better look."

She grabbed her binoculars and put them up to her eyes. She saw that it was Richard Rivers, Billy Goldstein, and Bobby Spinks, and without any hesitation or a second thought, she drove onto the school grounds saying, "I've got three of them. I have to take two of them down fast."

So, she grabbed that flexible, five-fingered, battery-operated gadget that blows out pins or nails. With it in her hand, Erin got closer to the three of them. She started to drive slower, all three of them were drunk. When they noticed that it was Erin, Billy Goldstein said loudly, "Look who we have here, one of the four little black girls. Oh, I forgot, there are three of you now. We're going to do you just like we did your sister."

As soon as he said that, the rage in Erin came out. She screamed, "Eye, eye, eye," and blew into that gadget towards him and those pin nails shot out. Two of them went right into each eye, the other went into the back of his mouth and two stuck him on his neck.

She never put the truck into park. She sped up just enough to jump out of the truck with her machete in her hand.

While Billy was now down on the ground bleeding from his eyes and neck, not able to do anything but rock from side to side, Bobby ran towards Erin holding up an empty liquor bottle in his hand, ready to hit her over the head screaming, "I'm going to kill you, you black bitch!"

Erin went into an upward spin and when she came down, she was behind Bobby. She kicked him in the middle of his back and you could hear something crack. When her foot was planted back on the ground, here came Richard. She felt him coming. She took that machete and rammed it right into his side. She pulled it out and then she said, "That's just the beginning of what I'm going to do to you. You're going to bleed a whole lot. It's going to sting and then you're going to get weak. But before you do, put both of them on the back of that truck and hurry up."

It was a struggle, but once Richard put the first person on the truck, which was Billy, who was still alive, but couldn't talk, Richard said to Billy, "Bro, she stabbed me in my side. I'm bleeding a whole lot."

Then Erin said, "None of you will ever see your family again. You should have left me and my sisters alone. Now you're all going to die!"

Richard walked over to Bobby. As he bent to get him off the ground, Bobby was laying there screaming out in pain, "My back! I can't feel my legs, you bitch!"

Erin yelled at Richard, "Step back, step back!" Then, she looked at Bobby and said, "That's the last time you will call me a bitch," and she snapped his neck.

"You killed him," Richard screamed.

"No, I didn't. He's just knocked out. I didn't come out here to kill anyone. I came to stop yall's asses from bullying me and my sisters," Erin said.

Erin looked at Richard with an evil eye and said, "And, you are next."

Holding his side, Richard tried to run. Erin sliced him right across the back of his neck and said, "You remember that?"

"Get your worthless ass on the back of the truck, and when you do I'm going to duct tape your hands and mouth. All four of you must have been cloned because y'all are heartless and you have no regards for human life. Well boys, real humans have no place for cloned generic humans," Erin said.

By this time, Richard was really getting weak, but Erin did not care; she did not help, and finally all three of them were on the back of the truck.

Erin asked Richard, "Where does Peter live?"

As she held the machete to his chest, "Please don't kill me," Richard pleaded.

"My family and I are grieving over my sister. Give me the address!" she demanded.

"12346 Summer Set Terrace, I'm hurting," Richard said.

"Well, goodbye Richard. Oh, you are going to get yourself and these animals off my truck," Erin said, as she took the machete and cut his shirt open and sliced across his chest, just deep for him to feel enough pain.

Erin wiped the blood off on their clothes, then lifted the gate on the truck. She got into the truck, grabbed the bottle of peroxide, poured it on the machete, and drove off heading to the location that she scoped out earlier.

When Erin reached that location, she backed up as close to the edge as she could. She put the truck in park and put the emergency brake on. Then she got out of the truck, climbed onto the back of the truck, stepped over those boys, and let the gate down. Then she said to Billy, "Well, you no good monster, we are at the Everglades. Do you know what lives here? Listen to this."

As Erin kicked the two boys off the back of the truck, Billy grabbed her leg and she grabbed his wrist and broke it.

Erin said, "I'm not going to kill. I'll let the snakes and the alligators and whatever else that lurks down there have fun, and so long you skuzzy, greiti, gratchi, grouchy."

Erin rolled Billy up with the plastic and blanket. She left his head uncovered, then she kicked him off the back of the truck. "Go be with your boys, you bastard," she said.

Erin drove home and went into the house. As she walked up the stairs, carrying her shoes in her hand, she noticed her dad was up.

He signed to her, "Where have you been? You are soaking wet. I thought that you were in your bed."

Erin signed back, "I was in the bed, Dad, but I could not sleep, so I went out for a while."

"Are you ok?" Aaron asked.

"I am good," she said, with a smile on her face. "I'll feel really good soon, and why would you ask that?"

"Because I am your father and I want to make sure that you are ok. Now, I'm not going to ask you about that 'I feel really good statement.' Go take that wet mess off, take a shower, put all of your defense tools away, clear your head, say your prayers, and go to bed. I'll see you in the morning," Aaron said.

After Aaron went back into his room and Erin went into her room, she took off her wet clothes and got into the shower. The entire time, while in the shower, she said to herself as she cried, "Des, they broke the chain. Three down and one to go. I miss you so much, sister. I'm so sorry that I was not close enough to you to help you. I'm really hurting right now, but it is going to be ok. I hurt because of what they did to you. You did not deserve any of it and now you are gone. I'm going to clock the last one, sis, that Peter Pitts. I'm going to slice that Mohawk right off of his head."

When Erin got out of the shower and put on her pajamas, she got into bed and a vision so clear of Destiny came to her. She sat up in the bed and said, "Des, you're here. You're not dead."

And the voice of Destiny said to Erin, "Only for a short time. I'm in a better place now. I love you, sister. I will always watch over you. You have always been my protector. I wish I could be here, but I'm ok. Let Mom, Dad, Junior, Ebony, and Chris know that I love them and I will forever be with them. Take care of yourself. I love you, Erin. Clock it."

And just like that, Destiny was gone and it gave Erin a feeling of relief. With a smile on her face, Erin said, "I love you too, Des, but it's not over yet." Then Erin laid back down and fell asleep.

The next morning when the sun came up, everyone was up in the house but Erin. Anita went to the stairs and yelled, "Erin, get up. We are getting ready to eat. Are you going to join us?"

Erin yelled back, "I'll be down in a minute."

Erin got out of bed and went into the bathroom. She washed her face and brushed her teeth. She put on another pair of sweatpants and a top, and then she went downstairs.

When Erin walked into the kitchen, Aaron looked at her and she looked at him, and she said, "Good morning everyone."

"How did you sleep last night?" he asked.

"I slept really well. Oh, Dad. After we talked and I went into my room, I got in the shower. You guys won't believe what happened!"

"What happened?" Aaron said.

"I saw Des. She came to me. It was so clear, just like I'm looking at all of you right now. She told me that she was ok and that she loves each one of you. She called everyone by name. After that, she left. It made me feel really good. You guys don't know how bad I was feeling. I could not help my sister when she needed me," Erin said.

"At that time, she needed all of us, but God stepped in and carried her home with him," Anita said.

"After I finish eating, I have to give Thurman a call to see if any of the tests have come back. If he is in the office and if any has come back, I think I'll ride to his job so that he can explain them to me," Aaron said.

"Well, if you go, I'll go with you," Anita said.

"Do you think you can stand it?" Aaron asked.

"Oh, I'm ok. My baby's shell is lying in the morgue, but I know her soul is with the Lord. He is carrying us through all of this. I know she is ok and we all just got confirmation when my child's sprit came to her sister last night to tell her that she's ok, so I'm ok," Anita said.

While sitting at the table eating, Erin said, "I've got to go out for a while, just to clear my head!"

"You want me to come with you?" Christian said.

"No, I just want to be alone for a while. I'm ok!" Erin answered.

"May I be excused?" Erin asked.

"Sure, baby. Be very careful out there," Anita said.

"Don't worry, Mom, I'll be very safe. I'll have my phone with me," Erin said.

When Erin excused herself from the table, she went upstairs and grabbed her numb chucks, her machete, and her flexible, five-fingered, battery-operated gadget. She walked down the stairs and yelled to her family and said, "I'll be back," and out the door she went.

This time she got into the car that she and her sisters shared. While walking to the car, Erin said to herself, "Three down and one to go."

Erin started the ignition. She thought to herself, "12346 Summer Set Terrace, here I come."

She started driving down the street, looking for that black jeep with the dent on the front bumper and the skeleton skull sticker on the back. Erin saw a black jeep parked at one of the convenience stores on the other side of the street, so she pulled into the gas station, up to a pump. Erin got out of the car and started washing her window, as she looked across the street, trying to see who got into the jeep. First, she washed the back window and then she dipped the squeegee into the bucket that had the windshield washing liquid in it and started on the front window. Just as she put the squeegee onto the glass, Peter Pitts came out of the store.

Erin's heart started racing as she looked at him. She quickly got back into her car. With the liquid running down the glass, Erin turned on the wipers and waited for her clearance to drive onto the road. She kept her eyes on that black jeep. The light turned red, "Good. Now I can get right up on him," Erin said.

As Erin got closer to the intersection, she was the third vehicle in the left lane. She knew that the black jeep had to turn left. When the light changed and they both turned left, Erin moved over into the lane next to the jeep.

They drove about a mile before coming to the next intersection. When they stopped at the next light, Erin's car and the black jeep would be the first cars to go when the light changed.

While sitting at the light, Erin stared at Peter Pitts with a very evil look. He turned and looked at her. The look on his face clearly showed that he was startled.

With their windows down, Erin said, "Follow me and show me how bad you think you are, Peter Pitts, just me and you punk."

Peter Pitts did just that. He followed Erin all the way to the same spot that she dumped his friends.

Erin stopped her car and put it in park. She got out of her car with her numb chucks stuck down in the back of her pants and her machete was hanging on the side of her.

While Peter was getting out of his truck, she pulled the numb chucks out and wacked him on his head. He turned around fast and started swinging. She moved to the side and kicked him. He ran towards her and Erin did a back-flip twirl, with her left foot almost on the ground, and with her right foot, she kicked him in the face. Now his mouth was bleeding. Erin ran closer to where she wanted to push Peter over the edge and he chased her. Peter caught up to Erin and grabbed her from behind around her neck. Erin flipped him and slammed him to the ground.

His legs dangled over the edge. He grabbed Erin by her ankle. Erin lost focus because his weight was pulling her very close towards the edge.

Erin started thinking of Destiny. Her thoughts were so intense that she could see flashbacks of when Destiny yelled for help the night that she was killed, and then she could hear Destiny saying, "I am protecting you now, sister, clock him."

When Destiny's voice said, "Clock him," Erin's focus returned. She pulled that machete out and with one swing, Erin cut off his hand. Then she took the hand from around her ankle, threw it over, and said, "Now you are with your good for nothing friends, and take your nasty hand with you."

Erin ran back to her car and started driving home really fast. She got home in no time. When she walked into the house, Aaron looked at her. She smiled back at him and then she walked upstairs.

Minutes later, Aaron went up the stairs. Erin's door was open. He walked into her room as she cleaned her machete with peroxide. Aaron got Erin's attention as he started signing, "I am almost afraid to ask you what you did because I know that you would not rest until you made those boys pay for what they did to you and your sisters, especially what they did to Des; but four wrongs don't make it right. But, I have to know. What did you do, Erin?"

Erin signed to her dad, "I did not kill anyone. When you saw me cleaning off my machete, I was wiping off the blood from Peter Pitts's hand!"

"Ok, blood, his hand, can you explain that to me, please?" Aaron asked.

"When I left the house, I went looking for Peter Pitts because he was the last one. I saw him coming out of the convenience store and I pulled up next to him at the light. I called him a punk and told him to follow me and show me how bad he is. So he followed me to the Everglades and that's where they all are," Erin explained.

"So what you are telling me is that all four of them are in the Everglades?" Aaron said.

"Yes sir, all four of them, Dad. Peter was the last one. He grabbed my ankle and he was pulling me to the edge, so I cut off his hand and he fell.

"You know, Dad, I don't feel sorry for those bums. They held hate for me and my sisters for many years and we never disrespected them. What they did to Des could have been all of us. They laughed at us like we were comedians telling jokes. They did lots of bad things to us daily, and no one did a thing at school even when we would report them. After a while you become tired of being bullied. No one should have to go through all that we did as young children. Now we're adults, bullied by the same four clowns, having to run home, looking over our shoulders. I found no humor in having security at the school to protect us. They tried to kill Chris and me. They vandalized our car. I guess that was so we couldn't get away. The media came to our home the night Des was killed and we haven't heard anything since, not even a call. Why? Because it was a black girl and they were white boys. That will never make it right. We are God's children, and for anyone to have the hate in them that they had for us, the devil is a liar, and I showed all of them. They had to be clocked and sent back to the pit of hell. You see, they didn't care what the laws are. They did what they wanted to do because they knew that their white parents and those white officials would protect them. I couldn't imagine having a family and I couldn't protect my children from being bullied daily. So no, I don't feel sorry, as a matter of fact, I am relieved, I feel good, I am happy," Erin explained to Aaron.

"Woo, pumpkin, you got a lot off your chest. I am happy to know that you are ok and that you have peace within. You know when they realize those guys are missing, the police are going to come here and I'm going to let them take you. But, I want you to say nothing and I will be there to get you out. Your mother and I are not hurting financially at all. This will add on to all the other lawsuits that are going to be presented after Destiny's funeral!" Aaron said.

"Oh, I know, Dad. They haven't seen a mental person until they see me. They don't want to mess with me and they have no evidence, none at all. It's ok. Let them come," Erin said.

"I don't want them hurting you by trying to medicate you in any way. I'm going to defend you, if it comes to that. But, I really don't think that it will. You will be ok!" Aaron said.

Aaron stood up to leave Erin's room. He signed, "Your mom is going to get an earful tonight. Oh, and I forgot to say, I called everyday asking if those boys have been picked up. I agree with what you said. It's a black-white thing. They have all of Peter Pitts's information, and not one time did they pick him up to question any of them. I am not happy that you did what you did. The chances you took could have gotten you killed."

"Just a reminder, during normal conversations, while in the house, the family will talk and not sign. But when we talk about any of this mess, we have to sign. Both Chris and Ebony know about our signing," Aaron said.

Then Aaron asked Erin, "Are you going with us to see Thurman?"

"If everyone else is going, then I'm coming along too," Erin said.

"Why don't you get dressed? We'll be leaving after lunch," Aaron said.

"Ok, Dad," Erin said.

Aaron left the room and walked down the stairs. When he went into the family room where Anita, Ebony, and Christian were, Chris looked at Aaron and signed to him saying, "What is going on? We know Erin did something."

With a very serious look on Aaron's face, he signed back saying, "I'm not talking about anything right now and none of you are to discuss what you may think with anyone."

Aaron felt that he could now speak out loud without signing, so he said, "Destiny's murder is being investigated and we are not going to talk about it with anyone. Now, have the police caught those boys who snatched Destiny? I don't know. Have they called the house phone or my cell phone with any updates? Nope, we have not seen those four boys and we don't want to see them. After we have lunch, we are going to talk with Thurman to see if all the tests have come back. Ebony, you and Christian go upstairs and get ready so we can leave after lunch."

Both Ebony and Christian said, "Ok, Dad."

Anita and Aaron prepared lunch for the family. While in the kitchen, Anita said, "I know we have a lot to talk about when we go to bed!"

"Oh yes, we do," Aaron answered.

After the family sat and ate lunch together, they left the home and headed to the morgue to talk with Thurman. While they were riding, Anita said, "All that has been going on, I think you all forgot that Junior will be home tomorrow!"

"Come on, Nita, we do have a lot on our plate, but I have not forgotten about Junior, I'll be happy to see our son," Aaron said.

"We have not forgotten. Have we Chris and Erin?" Ebony asked.

"Nope, I need my brother home with me right now," Erin said.

"Me too," Chris said.

"Well, you will have your brother home with you in the morning," Anita said.

When they got out of the car, Aaron asked, "Do we need to see Des again?"

"You know, God has really given us the strength. We lost a child. Her death is being investigated. We are waiting on the final autopsy reports to come back. She came to Erin and told her that she's ok, and I believe that. If you all want to, then yes, we will see her. Or maybe we can wait when we start funeral arrangements soon," Anita said.

"Ok, let's go on in," Aaron said.

So the family went into the building and asked to see Thurman. While they sat waiting, Jeff came into the waiting area.

"Hey family, how are you all holding up? I've been stopping by every other day to see if anything on my niece has come back!" Jeff said.

"It's been two weeks now. That's why we are here. Oh, Erin wants to talk with you for a second," Aaron said.

Erin looked at Aaron and said, "I do."

"Yes, you do," Aaron answered.

"Oh, that's right, Uncle Jeff. I do want to speak with you," she said.

"Should we go outside?" Jeff asked Erin.

"Yeah, I think we should," Erin answered.

So Jeff and Erin walked outside and stood on the steps of the building.

Jeff said, "So, what's up?"

"Uncle Jeff, did you and the other police officers look for those boys?" Erin asked.

"To be honest with you, Erin, I know those boys should have been caught the same night, but because they are white and Destiny is black, it wasn't a priority and we are assigned in areas that are not around those boys. But, I'll tell you this, Brian, Marques, Tyree, and I are still looking for them. We have a plan for them," Jeff said.

"Uncle Jeff, you don't have to look for them anymore. They are gone," Erin said.

"Gone, what do you mean gone?" Jeff asked.

"We don't have to worry about them anymore. They are all in the Everglades, and I took care of them for all of us," Erin said.

"What, by yourself?" Jeff said.

"Yes, Uncle," Erin said.

"All four of them? Ok, tell me niece, what did you do?" Jeff asked.

"Well, I went out the night that it rained. I saw three of them on the playground. The same grounds they attacked all of us and the same grounds where they killed Destiny. They had big nerve to go back to that location. I did not kill any of them. It was tough, but I just kicked them. I broke enough bones on them. I got them to the point they were begging me to stop. I hurt them so bad and I kicked three of them down into the Everglades that night. And Peter Pitts, I got him this morning. I wanted him bad. I think he was the leader of them all," Erin said.

"Don't talk about this to anyone. We will talk later on this. But when a missing person report is filed, the police may come to question you, maybe the whole family. Just be cool, girl, you are a bad lady. I guess you clocked them," Jeff said.

When Jeff's and Erin's conversation ended, they went back into the building; but by the time they went back in, the family had gone in the back to talk with Thurman. The cameras saw them and they were buzzed into the office area.

When Jeff and Erin entered the room, Thurman said, "Come on in and take a seat. We wanted to wait until you both joined us. Most of the tests have come back. Aaron, I did make copies of everything I have for your records. Now, I will explain to you what every test shows and I must say that some of what I have to say is graphic. Do you think that you can stand hearing it? Are you ready to hear it?"

Thurman looked at everyone in the room and everyone looked at each other. Some of them nodded their heads and the others responded and said, "We're ready."

Thurman started out saying, "The cause of Destiny's death was a broken neck. Under her nails were hair and skin tissue of four different individuals, and one of them tested positive to be that of Peter Pitts. The other three samples should arrive in the morning. There was sperm inside and around her vaginal area and also in her mouth. Destiny was bruised around her wrists and ankles and this was caused by her being held down. She also had bruises and defensive wounds caused by her fighting back. That's all I have right now, any questions?"

"So Thurman, do you think that tomorrow the last of the tests will be in your office?" Aaron asked.

"Yes, I do believe they will!" Thurman answered.

"Good. Now we can start making funeral arrangements for our baby," Aaron said, as he looked at Anita.

And then Aaron looked back at Thurman and said, "Will you call Nita or me when the final tests arrive?"

"I sure will," Thurman said.

"We are expecting lots of family to arrive in town this week for the girls' graduation. I feel while they are here, we can have the funeral. One day next week will be good, and that way it will save on travel," Aaron said.

After the family met with Thurman, they did want to see Destiny again, so they viewed her body and then they left to go home.

While Jeff and the family were talking outside of the building, Christian said, "I'm happy to know that Des will finally be laid to rest soon. She has been in the morgue, seems like forever!"

"Yes, baby. It does seem like a long time; but we had to wait for the investigation to be finalized," Anita said.

Jeff said to Aaron, "What's you all's plan when you leave here?"

"Right now, we are going home. You know my son will be home in the morning, so we are getting ready for him. It's been a while since we've seen him!" said Aaron.

"Well, if you don't mind, I'd like to come along so that we can talk. Why don't you ride with me?" Jeff said.

So Aaron rode in Jeff's car, and Anita drove the family's vehicle. Ebony, Christian, and Erin rode with her.

Jeff and Aaron discussed the disappearances of the four guys and how they thought things would turn out. They both talked about the worst thing that could happened is that Erin could be arrested under suspicion. But with no evidence at all, she would have to be released.

When the family arrived home, to their surprise, Junior was at home waiting for them. The girls jumped out of the car and ran over to him. They each gave hugs and kisses, then Junior walked over to Anita with his arms open wide. With tears in Anita's eyes, they gave each other a big, long hug.

Aaron and Jeff walked towards them and said, "Is this just something for the ladies? What about fathers and uncles, we don't get hugs?" Then Junior and Aaron hugged each other very tight. After their embrace ended, Junior looked at Jeff and said, "Jeff, or should I say Uncle Jeff? Junior and Jeff shook hands and hugged each other.

Anita said, "Come on, let's go in the house."

Then Aaron said, "Don't forget, if we discuss anything about Destiny's investigation, we have to sign because we don't know if the house or the phones are tapped."

So they all walked into the house and Junior took his things up to his room. When he came back down and turned the TV on, the news was on, and they all heard, "Coming up next. The families of three young men who have not been seen in two days are asking for your help."

When everyone heard that, they all looked at each other and Aaron said, "Probably a boating accident somewhere. It happens all the time!"

After the commercial, the news resumed. They started with the story on the missing young men. "Three families desperately need your help. If anyone knows the whereabouts or have seen Richard Rivers, Bobby Spinks, or Billy Goldstein, take a good look at their photos, report it to the police. They were all last seen leaving their homes two days ago. Now these young men, along with a fourth male, were always together. You may remember the assaults on two sisters and vandalism of their car here at the university. Sources believe that these four young men played a part in this. Also, you may remember the murder of Destiny Jackson, who was one of those sisters, just less than one month ago. Sources also tell us that these four young men were involved in that unsolved murder and that these four quadruplets were bullied by the same four young men as children, back in Washington, D.C. If you know anything, please contact the police tip hotline at 1-308-915-1206. If your tip leads to an arrest, you can receive up to an $80,000 reward. Reporting live from APX news, I'm Wanda Curtis."

When that clipping went off, there were fingers signing and mouths opened. Jeff walked over to turn the radio on to distort sounds, so that it will allow them to talk.

Then Junior opened his mouth saying, "Missing, the same four bullies. I can bet anyone in this room we are going to see more about those boys on the news and you can count the number of times they reported the murder of my sister. And how hard did they try to find the killers?"

Then Junior looked at Erin and gave lip gesture saying, "You clocked them, didn't you?"

Erin nodded her head yes.

Christian and Ebony looked at each other, while everyone looked at them. Then Christian said, "Why are we the last ones to know about all of this?"

"If you don't know about it, then you can't speak about it," Aaron said.

Ebony looked at Anita. "Tell me, Mom!" she said.

Anita said, "I can't tell what I don't know!"

Then Ebony looked at Aaron, with a concerned sounding voice. She said, "Dad, I can't believe you would keep this from Chris and me. We will never say a word to anyone. We are a team and Destiny was a part of us. Erin is a part of us. We will never do anything that will cause them hurt, harm, or danger. Dad, you know that!"

"I know, pumpkin. Everything happened so fast, from the injuries at school to Destiny's murder. Now we have graduation to focus on and plan my child's funeral. A lot has happened," Aaron said.

"Ok, Dad, we know that Erin clocked them, but we don't know how she did it. Mama, can you tell us what happened?" Aaron Jr. said, as he looked at Anita.

"Baby, I don't know. Your dad, Erin, and I'm assuming Jeff, they are the ones to ask. We all are waiting to hear what happened. I'm sure we will know soon. Won't we, honey?" Anita said, as she looked at Aaron.

Then Erin said, "Ok, Uncle Jeff, we are family and we stick together through thick and thin. I want to tell what happened a few nights ago. I left the house looking for all four of those boys. I drove around for a while and something told me to go to the schoolyard. That's where Bobby, Richard, and Billy were drinking. It made me so mad because this was the same place where they attacked me and my sisters, and then brought one back to rape, torture, and kill. I had to clock them.

"When I pulled up on the school grounds, Billy said, 'Oh, one of the four little black bitches.' Excuse me, Mom, Dad, and Uncle Jeff. Then he said, 'Oh, I forgot, it's three of you now. We are going to do you like we did your sister.' I could not believe the rage that came over me. I took that five-finger blower and blew it right into his face. The pins went into both eyes, his neck, and his mouth. When he fell to the ground, Bobby ran to help him. Then he ran over to me with his empty liquor bottle yelling, 'I'll kill you.' Excuse me again, 'You little black bitch.' I went into an upward sparrow spin and came down. I kicked his back and snapped his spine. Then came Richard. I took the machete and rammed it into his side. I made him give me Peter's address and made him put the other boys on the truck. Oh, don't worry, there was no mess. Then while I was in the shower that night, Destiny came to me. It was just like she was actually standing in my room. She told me that she was ok and to tell everyone that she loves them and she said, 'Clock them.' That really made me feel good seeing her, but I was not finished. I had to get that Mohawk.

"So the next day, I went driving looking for that jeep. When I spotted it at the convenience store, I pulled into the gas station across the street pretending to be cleaning my windshields. When he came out, I got into the car and caught up with him at the next light. He looked over at me and I said, 'Follow me, show me that you can beat my tail, punk.' So he did, and I led him right to the Everglades. That's where he and his buddies are. I just want to say, I'm happy they are out of our lives; and if I go to jail, I will be ok. I have a plan for that as well!"

With a firm voice, one that you can hear every letter pronounced, Anita said, "Jail, oh, so you have a plan? And what's your plan, Miss Missy? Tell us about your plan! Go on, tell us! We all would like to hear this!"

"Well, if the police comes to arrest me, what's the reason? Suspicion of anger, the attitude that I showed towards what happened to Destiny. Yes, I am still angry; and Dad, don't you come and get me out. The parents of those boys are going to pay for all of this," Erin explained.

"You have to remember; these are four white boys we are talking about. You know how the law takes sides with white people," Jeff said.

"I know, Uncle Jeff, but what the law doesn't know is that I am very intellectual. I can speak five languages fluently, and besides that, my dad is one of the top lawyers in this state," Erin said.

"Well Erin, it seems like you have a plan, and a good one, if I must say so. AJ, she's been watching you," Jeff said.

After that was said, they heard breaking news on the TV, "Reporting live, we're at the Everglades where the truck, a black jeep belonging to that of missing Peter Pitts was spotted by a tourist, just a couple of hours ago, just behind me. You can see it being loaded up onto a flatbed tow truck. Where could these four young men be? Police are still looking for answers. If you know something, please call the tip line shown on the screen. Reporting live from APX news, I'm Wanda Curtis."

After that report, Jeff said, "Well, they are really looking for those boys. All of you know how to get in contact with me if you need me. I'm heading home and I'll call you later."

Each one of them said goodbye in their own way, whether it was see you later, talk with you later, or bye.

The next morning, while the Jacksons were enjoying each other, sitting, laughing, and having breakfast, suddenly a loud knock was on the door.

When the family heard that sound, Junior said, "You know who that is, nobody but the police."

"We are not going to start an argument or a big fuss. I told all of you that I can handle this. This is false arrest and that's another lawsuit. I just finished my breakfast. If you noticed, I ate extra. Now it's time for me to tell them nothing. Don't worry, I'm ok. Dad, don't get me out right away, wait until Tuesday!" Erin said.

"Tuesday, why wait until Tuesday? Today is Wednesday. Do you know that's six days away? I'm getting you out today. We are going to have lots of family coming out of town for you all's graduation and the funeral. Now, we have to prepare for court as well," Aaron said.

With a slow dragging, spoiled sounding voice, Erin said, "Dad, please. This is what I'm asking of you. My plan will work. If you can set up a court date for that day or Wednesday, the next day, I won't be in jail long. They will take me for a mental evaluation, watch!"

Aaron walked towards the door. He said, "I don't believe what you are asking of me. Your mom and I are going to do this, but if your plan falls through, I am going to step in and handle this myself."

He turned and opened the door. On the other side, standing on the porch were two white police officers. Aaron said, "Morning officers, how may I help you?"

One of the officers said, "Mr. Jackson, I am Officer Freshman."

"I know who you are. We met in court a few times. We didn't call for police presence. How may we help you?" Aaron asked.

"Mr. Jackson, we have a warrant to arrest your daughter Erin Jackson for the disappearance of Peter Pitts, Richard Rivers, Billy Goldstein, and Bobby Spinks," Officer Freshman said.

"A warrant to arrest my child for the disappearance of the same four boys who raped and murdered my child. You have got to be jockeying me. So, what you are telling me is that none of you officers could find these four guys, but my daughter could and now they are missing?" Aaron said.

Aaron put out his hand and said, "Let me see those papers."

The officer handed the papers to Aaron. As he read the papers, he found lots of mistakes in the wording and spelling, so he said to the officers, "Where's my copy?"

"Well sir, we didn't bring an extra copy with us," the officer answered.

"Well, if you don't mind, I'd like to make a copy of this for my records. I'm sure you understand. Just wait right here and it will only take a few seconds," Aaron said.

While Aaron ran to the office to makes copies, he was thinking, "I should be nervous, upset, angry, and afraid. My child is going to jail and I'm not putting up a fuss. I know she can handle herself. I'll have this mess expunged, sue the state, and go back home."

Aaron came back with the papers and handed them to the officer and said, "Thanks," and then he turned and called Erin's name.

When Erin walked towards Aaron, the whole family came with her. Anita, Ebony, and Christian were crying. Through the evil look on Erin's face, she also had tears in her eyes. They all hugged Erin and gave her kisses.

Anita told Erin, "I love you, don't be afraid. Just pray and we will be down to see you."

Aaron said, "Be strong, pumpkin, I love you."

Junior said, "Clock them, sis," in French.

The officer asked Erin, "Ma'am, will you turn around so that I can place the cuffs on your wrists?"

Erin turned and looked at her family with a smirk grin on her face. Then she turned back around once the cuffs were placed on her wrists.

Erin was arrested for the disappearance of the four boys and the state had no evidence. They were going on Erin's character and the way she expressed herself towards all that has taken place. People were saying that she showed a wicked side and they believed that she could be the one who caused their disappearance.

Junior said, "Now that the police has arrested Erin, just listen to what I'm saying, we are going to see breaking news and just watch the number of people that will be outside of the jailhouse. Why? Because she's black."

When Erin arrived at the jailhouse, there were lots of news reporters and cameramen, all standing outside of the building, along with the parents of all the boys and other protesters, who were yelling out, "You killed them. Where are they? Murderer," and other words. But, Erin never changed her facial expression.

A reporter asked Erin, "Miss Jackson, what happened to the four boys?" Then she put the mic up to Erin's mouth, but Erin continued to walk as she was being led.

Back at the Jackson's house, breaking news came on the TV. "What did I tell you? Look at all of those people standing outside. I'm telling you if one of them spit or put their hand on Erin, I'm going down there myself. Because those boys are white, see what they do? They are going to be shocked when they find out that they have nothing," Junior said.

Once they got into the building, Erin did everything like she said she would, nothing. Detective Arthur Fisher took Erin into a room to question her and she said nothing. Three different detectives tried and they got nowhere. Each detective that went into the room said, "Good afternoon, Miss Jackson, I have a few questions to ask you."

Each time, they were carrying the photos of the four missing boys. Some of the questions asked by the detectives as they showed the pictures were, "Do you know these four men? Have you seen these four men? Are you a violent person? Did you kill these four men? Do you know where they are? Where are these four men? Are you deaf? Can you talk?"

Erin was in the interrogation room for a long time, but the detectives got nowhere.

Back at the Jackson's house, Aaron was pacing the floor back and forth saying, "I should not have listened to her. We should have gone down to the jailhouse with her. What I need to do is go down to the jail and get my baby out!"

"No, what you need to do is come and sit down beside me. Erin has a plan and we don't know what it is, but she begged you to let her do this. Now, I don't want my child in this mess either; but I think it will all turn out ok," Anita said.

"You know what, Dad? We are not hurting for money, but all of us are getting ready to receive a little extra. And with our college degrees, we can maybe start our own business or maybe a center for people who have been bullied or raped. And we can do it in Destiny's honor," Christian said.

"I was going to say money is not everything, but that is a good idea. I wonder how Erin is holding up," Aaron said.

Ebony said, "Has anyone talked with family members to let them know what is going on and what's going to take place in the next few weeks or so?"

Aaron pulled out his cell phone and said, "Let me give Mama an update on what's going on. I know they are worried!"

Anita walked over to get the house phone, she started singing out loud, *"Yield Not to Temptation."*

Then Aaron started singing, *"Life's Railway to Heaven."*

Then Ebony sang, *"The Battle is the Lord's."* Then she said, "We are going to make it through all of this, Mom and Dad."

While Aaron and Anita were both on the phone talking with family, Chris looked at Junior and said, "What now, brother?"

"Right now, we just have to play the waiting game with Erin. I do know that the justice system for this state is messed up. You have four white boys who bullied four black girls, all the way back in elementary school. Somehow, as young adults, the four white boys ended up in the state where the four black girls live and attended school. The four white boys continued to bully the four black girls and they went as far as doing bodily harm and destroying property. They all were told that their parents would be held accountable for their actions, but did that stop them? No. They went on and did what they wanted to do, raped and killed one of the black girls. Well, what I think is that their parents will pay dearly. And when I get the job of my dreams, all of those whites who hate blacks will see that there is a new sheriff in town, and he is not going to tolerate any of that kind of mess," Junior answered.

Back at the police station, every detective who tried to interview Erin got nowhere. So the four of them met outside of the room. They stood talking, trying to figure out how to get Erin to answer questions. They were wondering if she was deaf, if she had a mental problem, or if she was afraid to be where she was. They also wondered if Erin was one of the girls who was attacked at school. The detectives had no answers. What they agreed on was to have Erin stay the night at the jailhouse, try to question her in the morning, and then take her to the institution for a mental evaluation.

While the detectives stood in the hall talking, Erin could hear every word. She had to go to the restroom, so she walked over to the door and saw the ladies' room directly across the hall. Erin got the attention of the detectives, while looking at their name badges once again, to store them in her memory bank. They all looked at her, then she pointed her finger at the ladies' room.

Detective Myron Greyson said, "So, you have to go potty? You got to pee pee. Let me hear you ask."

While the others gave a little chuckling laugh, Erin made no change in her expression. She just walked over to the ladies' room, opened the door, and went in.

Detective Greyson said, "I should go in there." Detective Alexander McNeill dared him.

When they heard the toilet flush, Detective Greyson walked into the ladies' room. Erin had not come out of the stall, but she heard the door open. Her mind started to wonder, "What is going on?" She could hear Destiny saying, "Clock them."

When Erin walked out of the stall, there stood Detective Greyson. She didn't say a word. She walked over to the sink to wash her hands. She put the soap on her hands, then turned the water on. Detective Greyson stood there looking at Erin; and she looked at him through the mirror. When she turned the water off and walked to get a paper towel to dry her hands, Detective Greyson walked over by the paper towel holder also. Erin did not make any eye contact with him. But when she walked towards the trash can, Detective Greyson touched her on her butt. Erin grabbed his hand. She gave him an evil look, and then she bent his hand back so far, his fingers were touching his arm. You could hear the bones in his hand break.

While Detective Greyson screamed in agonizing pain, the other detectives ran to his defense. Detective McNeill franticly asked, "What happened?" as the injured Detective Greyson remained down on his knees, holding his wrist.

He said with a painful sounding voice, "I mistakenly touched her ass."

Detective McNeill's response was, "You did what?"

Detective Earley Eborn said, "Your hand is turning blue. You need to go to the hospital. We can't let this get out. We all can be suspended!"

"We can be sued and lose our jobs behind this. What reason do we have being in the ladies' room? We could have called for a female to assist the suspect. What are we going to do with the suspect while we're at the hospital?" Detective Alexander McNeill asked.

"We have no other choice but to take her with us," Detective Earley Eborn said.

So the detectives walked out the ladies' room and headed down the hall, along with Erin. Detective Alexander McNeill told Katie, the clerk at the desk, "We are taking the suspect to the mental institution and taking Detective Myron Greyson to the hospital. He had a fall. We think his hand is broken!"

They left the building and headed to the hospital. Erin had on no handcuffs and she knew the law. But all she had on her mind was clearing her name, making this an unsolved case, and suing the state for all that's coming to her and her family.

When they got to the hospital, Detective Eborn went into the back treatment area with Detective Myron Greyson. Detectives Arthur Fisher and Alexander McNeill sat out in the waiting area with Erin.

Meanwhile, a few minutes later, Erin's mom walked into the hospital. She saw Erin sitting with the two detectives. Dr. Anita Jackson walked swiftly over to Erin and said, "Are you alright?"

But before Erin could answer, Detective McNeill said to Anita, "Ma'am, you can't talk to her. She's in our custody!"

"I will talk to her whenever I want. She is my child. Why is she here?" Anita asked, with a firm voice.

"Well, ma'am, your daughter is ok. She is riding along with us. One of our detectives is being seen here," Detective Fisher answered.

Anita looked at the detective's name and said to him, "Well, Detective Arthur Fisher, if you don't mind, I'd like to speak with my daughter for a minute, if it's ok with you."

"Oh sure, go right ahead, Dr. Jackson," Detective Fisher answered.

Anita moved over a few chairs away from the detectives, with her back turned away from them, where they couldn't see the both of them signing. Anita asked Erin, "Are you ok?"

Erin said, "Yes."

"Why are you here?" Anita asked.

"Because I broke one of the detective's hand!" Erin answered.

Anita stretched her eyes and opened her mouth and said, "You broke the detective's hand?"

"Yes, I did. He touched my butt while I was in the ladies' room," Erin answered.

"While you were in the ladies' room? What was he doing in the ladies room with you?" Anita asked.

"I don't know, but when I came out of the stall, he was standing there after I washed my hands and dried them off. He touched my butt when I was putting the paper towel in the trash. I grabbed his hand and broke his wrist, but I'm ok," Erin said.

"You know, I don't like any of these plans. Do I need to call your daddy and have him to come and get you out of this mess?" Anita asked.

"No, Mom. You don't need to call Daddy. I told you my plan is going to work out. Please, let me do this. They are going to take me to the mental institution in the morning, so that's where I will be. These detectives don't know if I can talk because I have not said a word to them. You will know when it's time to get me," Erin said.

"I am so glad I came here when I did. Those dirty dogs! You will probably be here for a while. I am going to go into the back and make sure I get a copy of that record. I will be back. Look, another violation, no handcuffs. I love you, sweet pea," Anita said.

"I love you too, Mommy," Erin said.

Anita got up and went into the back. She saw Detective Earley Eborn, who was waiting. She walked over to the station and everyone knew her. They were happy to see her. They offered their condolences to her and asked how she was doing. She told them, "It has been tough for me and my family, but God is with us all the way." Then she said, "Look, I need a favor. The officer who is being treated, why is he here?"

Trisha, the nurse on duty (which was one of Anita's friends) said, "He said he fell and broke his hand, but from the x-rays, nearly every bone in his hand and wrist is broken, and that's his dominant hand. It looks like he won't be working for a long time. He's going to need a lot of reconstructive surgery on that hand. What is going on?"

"I can't tell you now, but you know how we talk. I have to bring you up to snuff when all this is over. It is too much to tell now," Anita said.

"Hey, I'll make a copy of his chart and take it home with me. I'll give you a call," Trisha said.

"Thanks, I'll talk with you then. I got to run upstairs and make sure all of my time is in," Anita said, as she left, heading to the Office of Human Resources.

A few moments later, Detective Earley Eborn came out and told Detectives Arthur Fisher and Alexander McNeill, who were sitting in the waiting area that, "It doesn't look good. Detective Greyson's fingers and wrist are crushed up. They are preparing him for surgery. The doctors are saying that he has a slim chance of ever using that hand much at all. They said it was a terrible fall." All three detectives looked over at Erin, as she looked at them.

Detective Arthur Fisher said, "Well, let's see how long the surgery is going to be. We can wait here for a while. I think we need to drop our suspect off at the mental institution tonight, instead of in the morning. What do you guys think?"

Detective McNeill said, "That's a good idea. Doesn't look like we are going to get anywhere with her."

Detective Eborn said, "This whole thing is messed up. We don't have the proper paperwork. All of us is going to be in for some real dunk down the road. Watch what I tell you."

Time ticked by and the wait seemed like forever. Erin's mom stopped back by the waiting area before she went home. The sun was starting to set, so she asked Detective Fisher, "Has my daughter eaten lunch or dinner?"

Detective Arthur Fisher answered, "Oh, no ma'am, we're taking her to the mental institution when we leave here. They will have food to give her!"

"So from the time the officers came to my house to arrest my child and took her down to the police station, for something we have nothing to do with or know anything about except for what we saw on the television, she hasn't even been given a cracker. Has she been offered water?" Anita boldly expressed.

"Well, Mrs. Jackson, she didn't ask. She doesn't talk," said Detective McNeill.

"Dogs don't talk, but their owners give them food and water. I'm glad I asked. Let me go get my child something to eat before I go home. Your department, the county, and this state have a lot they are going to answer for," Anita said.

Then she walked away and stopped. She turned around and said, "This is a big joke. I'm not going to go to the cafeteria and bring my child's food back. One of you is going to come down with us, so that we can sit at the table and eat. Now, I don't care who comes along to escort my baby; but one of you need to get up and we can head down to the cafeteria."

So Detectives Arthur Fisher and Alexander McNeill decided to go, while Detective Earley Eborn said he would wait, just in case anyone came with news about Detective Myron Greyson.

Down in the cafeteria, the detectives sat at a table and allowed Erin and her mom to go through the serving line to get their food.

While standing in the line, Anita said, "This is a real big mess. If I've never seen a mess before, this is it. What state do you know has laws that allow a black person, who is a suspect in the disappearance of four white guys, ride to the hospital with the detectives? The suspect breaks one of the detective's fingers and wrist and he tells the doctors that he fell. They did not feed the suspect. None of the paperwork is correct. The suspect is not wearing handcuffs, and now she's standing in the hospital's cafeteria with her mom getting food. A mess! I can write a book about the whole ordeal."

"Mom, my graduation is in two days," Erin said.

"I know, baby. You begged your dad not to come and get you out. Now if you are having a change of thought, I can call him right now and you can sleep in your bed tonight!" Anita said.

"No, but tell Dad to make sure I am out before Des's funeral. You know this is the first time I've talked since I left home, and when they take me to that mental institution, I'm not going to talk with them either," Erin said.

As Erin and her mom walked from the line getting their food, they sat at a table away from the detectives. That way they would be able to talk privately.

"You really have a plan, don't you? Whatever it is, I hope it pays off dearly. Like your dad said, 'I don't believe we let our child talk us into this,'" Anita said.

"I'm going to make sure we come to visit you as often as we can. You know with your graduation and all, the family that's coming, we are going to be very busy. Right after the graduation, we have to plan for the funeral. I hope your dad has gotten the call from Thurman. Enough about that right now, when you get to that institution, places like that will try to heavily medicate you. No, I'm driving to the institution right behind the detectives. I'll give Aaron a call and let him know what's going on. It will only be a few days that you will spend in there, four at the most, according to your plan," Anita said.

"Mom, you don't have to bring Grandma Henri or Grandma Les to visit me. I will be ok. Let them know I have a plan. But if they insist, wait for at least two days, then y'all can come," Erin said.

"Why two days?" Anita asked.

"Mom, please, I can't say right now. You will see in two days. You said that you and Dad agreed to my plan. Can we stick to the agreement?" Erin begged.

"Your dad and I had a dumb moment in thought to agree with this, with everything else that's going on in our family right now!" Anita said.

"Things will kind of be back to normal after all this is over. I'm wearing my graduation dress to Des's funeral. You know, Mommy, I miss her so much. When I come up against situations and I have to defend myself, I can hear Des's voice saying, 'Clock them,' and all of me transforms into defense mode," Erin said.

"You know we all miss her deeply, but I thank God for all of my children. I'm not going to cry because He has been here to comfort us through all of this. Things will never be totally normal because a piece of my four and one is physically gone. I'm going to have Destiny dressed in her graduation dress also. I think it was an awesome idea when you girls went shopping for your graduation dresses and you all decided to dress alike. I'm sure Ebony and Chris will wear their dresses too. What do you mean, when you come up against situations, you hear Des's voice?" Anita asked.

"You know, Mom, I really do. It's just like when I said she was in my bedroom. I don't know, maybe she's protecting and watching over me right now. I heard her voice with those boys, and I heard it again when I was in the bathroom at the jailhouse. Like they say, I guess she's watching my back, keeping me alert," Erin explained.

Detective Eborn came over and asked, "Are you finished eating?"

Anita answered, "Yes. We are finished."

Anita told Erin, "Let's put our trays on the belt and go see what's going on."

So Erin and Anita walked to put their trays on the belt. As they got closer, they could hear Detective Eborn telling Detectives Fisher and McNeill that Detective Greyson will have to stay the night in the hospital because of the swelling in his arm, and that he will have screws in his fingers and wrist for a while.

Detectives Fisher and McNeill just shook their heads with a concerned look on their faces.

"Well gentlemen, are we ready to take my daughter to the mental institution?" Anita said.

The three detectives sat, looking up at Anita. Then she said, "Oh yes, I'll be following behind you. You see, this is my baby, very precious cargo. Her dad and I have already lost one child. We can't stand losing another one," Anita said.

Detective Fisher stuttered, as he said, "Oh sure, ma'am, that's fine, we're ready."

Detective Fisher said to his colleagues, "Come on, guys. Let's roll."

So they left the hospital and headed to their cars. Anita gave Aaron a call.

He answered his cell phone. "Hey, honey. I got the final papers from Thurman. Are you still at the hospital?"

"I'm leaving now. You won't believe this. When I walked into the hospital, I parked over by the emergency entrance and you know I never park on that side. I walked through the doors and I saw Erin sitting with two detectives. So I went over to her and asked them if I can speak with my child. She and I moved away from them to talk. She broke one of the detective's fingers and wrist because he came into the ladies' room while she was in there. He touched her butt and she broke his hand. You know I have more to tell you when I get home. I'm following them to the mental institution now. I'll see you when I get home," Anita said.

"Well, how is Erin?" Aaron asked.

"She appears to be ok. We talked while we ate dinner," Anita answered.

"Ate dinner?" Aaron asked.

"Yes, I told you I have a story to tell you when I get home," Anita answered.

"So, they took the handcuffs off her and let her sit and have dinner with her mother?" Aaron asked.

"She's not even wearing handcuffs!" Anita said.

"What! What did you say? Those folks are really messing up. They don't know what they are doing, and I should have not let my daughter leave this house with those fools," Aaron said.

"Remember sugar, our child is on a mission and she don't want us to come visit her at the institution for two days. I told you I have a lot to talk with you about when I get home," Anita said.

"Ok, babe. I can't wait to hear all of it. Call me if you need me and be safe. I love you," Aaron said.

"You know I will call you and I'll be safe. I love you too. Talk with you later," Anita said, as the call ended.

They arrived at the mental institution. They all got out of the car to go inside. At the check-in location, a man who appeared to be very old was sitting. His name was Jason. So they walked up to the desk. Jason looked up and said, "Hey guys, what can I do for you tonight?"

Detective Earley Eborn said, "Jason, we have one to be evaluated."

"Ok, what's the name?" Jason said.

Detectives Fisher, McNeill and Eborn all looked at each other, and Detective McNeill said, "I don't have the papers."

"Neither do I. All I know is the last name is Jackson. Jason, give us a minute," Detective Fisher said.

"Sure, take as long as you like. I'll be here all night long," Jason answered.

"Oh, for God's sake, I don't believe this. You men have got to be nervous. I would hate to think that this is the way you perform daily," Anita said.

Anita stepped up to the glass window and said, "Excuse me, Jason, Erin Jackson is her name."

"Are you Erin Jackson?" Jason asked.

"No, I'm her mother," Anita answered.

Then, Anita stepped away from the window as the detectives walked back over to the window.

"Is she on any medication?" Jason asked, as he looked up at the detectives. He saw them looking at each other.

They stepped aside and Anita walked up again and said, "No, Erin is not on any medication."

Jason asked, "Is the patient violent?"

Detective Eborn walked up and said, "Well, she broke my partner's wrist!"

"So you can tell it now, Detective Earley Eborn? Don't play with me! The hospital's records show that your partner had a fall. It's ok to lie for each other, when your job is on the line. Your department came to my home and got my child this morning, and it's almost morning again. You questioned her all day. I'm sure, up until she broke your partner's wrist for touching her butt. And you don't even know her name. She's not a violent young lady. My entire family will defend ourselves whenever we have to!" Anita said.

Anita looked at Jason and said, "No, Jason. Erin is not a violent person!"

Jason said, "Well, I say can be defensive when provoked. Is that ok, ma'am?"

"All of this is giving me a sour taste in my mouth. Yes, that's fine, Jason. Oh, and I know most institutions want to give medications to the patients, but don't even try it! She doesn't take any medication, so don't give her any. Is that understood?" Anita boastfully said.

"Yes ma'am, understood. Let me note no medication to be given," Jason answered.

After the paperwork was filled out, Jason called for someone to come and show Erin to her room. Anita waited because she wanted to see what kind of room Erin would be staying in. They all sat down and waited for ten minutes before someone came to get Erin; and when her name was called, both she and Anita stood up.

Anita said, "Hi, this is Erin. I'm her mother. I just want to come back and maybe take a short tour, maybe see her room or one similar, also the bathroom, kitchen, the sitting area, and wherever the patients are allowed. Is that ok?" Anita asked.

The night attendant, whose name was Kala, looked at Jason. With his back turned, he threw his hand up and said, "Whatever, go right ahead."

Then Kala said, "Right this way."

"Thank you, Kala," Anita said.

As they walked down the hall, Kala pointed out each room. Anita stuck her head in each room to look inside. For the rooms that didn't have the lights on, she turned them on to look inside. Then they went to Erin's room number 122. Anita walked inside. She made sure it was clean. She did a finger inspection for dust. She checked the bathroom and bed sheets. After she toured the facility, Anita thanked Kala for her time and said, "I'd better go home."

Anita gave Erin a hug and said, "I love you, pumpkin," and Erin signed back saying, "I love you too."

When Anita went back to the lobby area, the three detectives were still sitting. She said, "You men must be off work by now. I guess you're trying to get your story together. You all have a good night." And she walked out of the building.

"That lady must have read our minds," Detective Fisher said.

"Hopefully, by the time the truth comes out, we are all retired. I'm not going to tell them that we stood outside the ladies' room, while one of our detectives just walked in the ladies' room, when we could have called for a lady to assist her," said Detective McNeill.

"I know we better think of something. Oh, we're just going to say that Detective Greyson took a nose-dive fall and broke his hand in the process. How does that sound?" said Detective Earley Eborn.

"Sounds good to me," said Detective Fisher.

"I think we can get away with that, now let's head back," Detective McNeill said.

When Anita got home, Aaron was on the bed watching TV. "You're still up?" she asked.

Aaron said, "I know you didn't think that I was going to sleep while my wife was out and about. You see I have not taken off my clothes, but now I can. So tell me about your day. I want to hear everything. So our child broke the detective's wrist?"

"Quiet, so I can tell you the whole story," Anita said.

Anita took off her clothes and put on her nightgown and climbed onto the bed and said, "Ok, so Erin broke the detective's wrist because he touched her butt. First, he should not have been in the ladies' room!"

"Was he in the ladies' room while she was using the bathroom?" Aaron asked.

"No, she said after she flushed the toilet, that's when she heard the door open, and when she walked out there, he was standing in the ladies' room. So she washed her hands and when she went to throw the paper towel in the trash, that's when he touched her butt. Baby, Erin said when she grabbed his hand, the grip that she had on it broke his wrist and most of his fingers. When I went to the hospital, I told you about what happened when we arrived at the mental institution. The detectives called themselves checking Erin in and not one of the three detectives knew her first name. They stood their looking stupid. I had to check her in. When the question came up asking if Erin is violent, the detective quickly said, 'Well, she broke my partner's wrist!' But, at the hospital, they said he fell. They were covering up for one of them!

"Oh yes, you know I had to step in. I said, 'So, at the hospital, you can lie for your partner to cover y'all's butts; but here, you want to make my child appear to be violent. Oh, the truth will be told.' Then I turned and looked at Jason. He's a little old white man who appeared to be worn out. And do you know after I toured the facility, those three detectives were still sitting out in the waiting area? I said to them, 'I know you must be off work by now. Oh, I guess you have to get your lies together before you go back,' and I walked out," Anita said.

"You told them that they were getting their lies straight?" Aaron asked.

"I sure did and walked out. I almost forgot, Erin said that she did not want any visitors for two days!" Anita said.

"Why is that?" Aaron asked.

"Well, just like she said before she left home, with that whiny voice, 'Mommy, please.' You are the one who first agreed to let her handle whatever mission she's on, but let me get off that and say this while it's on my mind. I think we should take Destiny's body home where all of our family is, bury her there, and have something small here for her friends. What do you think?" Anita said.

"I agree. I thought about that and planned on talking with you. I even went as far as us moving back to South Carolina. I can still have my firm here and the one back home as well. We can come visit, but I don't want to stay here. Too many unhappy things went on. I just want to restart what we started back in our school days, nothing but love and fun times," Aaron said, as he looked into Anita's eyes and gave her a big kiss.

"I want to mention to Ebony and Chris that I think they should wear their graduation dresses to the funeral," Anita said.

Aaron gave Anita a strange look.

Then she said, "That's right, when the girls went shopping for their dresses for graduation, they all bought the same dress and that's what Des is going to have on," Anita explained.

"I think that's an awesome idea. Now you have to find something that will blend in with their colors. Junior and I will find matching shirt and tie that will blend in. And after all this is over and God orders our steps, we will open up some type of organization in Destiny's honor. If I must say so, that child of mine, she's no dummy. No sir, not by a long shot!" Aaron said.

Erin plotted and planned her game all the way to the end. She did not write anything down or tell anyone what her plans were. But her family knew that something was going to take place. She knew that if she refused to eat at the mental institution, they could not hold her and let her starve to death.

While Erin was locked down in the mental institution for three days, refusing to eat and talk, the first day she was lying down on the bed with her back towards the door when she heard someone entering the room quietly. She heard Destiny's voice saying, "Clock them." Just when she heard that voice, Erin swung her legs around in a circular motion, knocking down the two workers. One was a lady and the other was a man. They entered the room to give Erin a shot, something to make her talk.

The needle dropped out of the nurse's hand. Erin kicked the male orderly in his face. The nurse ran and so did the orderly, but not before he saw blood.

Erin quickly grabbed the needle and hid it inside a piece of the dresser that was not tightly connected. Then Sam, the orderly, and Nancy, the nurse on duty, went down to the office where the person in charge for the evening was sleeping at the time.

Sam called out his name, "Percy, hey Percy, you need to wake and look at me!"

Percy opened his eyes and said, "What happened to you?"

"I was kicked in the face by the Jackson girl!" Sam said.

"Well, that's the way y'all do each other," Percy said.

"What do you mean y'all, Percy? Whites aren't always right. That's what y'all want people to believe. Everyone in this building knows that you don't like blacks, but that's not stopping the world from going around.

Nancy and I went into the Jackson girl's room to give her the medication, but she ran me and Nancy out of there," said Sam.

"Nancy, did you give her the shot?" Percy asked.

"No, before we could even get to her, she started kicking and I dropped the needle filled with the medication in the room," she said.

"Y'all know that she's the one who's being charged for those four missing young guys, don't you?" Percy said.

"That girl is not the reason why those guys are missing," Sam said.

"How do you know, Sam?" Percy asked.

Then Nancy also said, "How do you know?"

"This goes out to the both of you. I don't know, and how can you say that she is?" Sam said.

"That's why we need her to talk, so we can find out. Come with me. I'll hold her down," Percy said.

"Wait a minute. Let me wash my face," Sam said.

When Erin closed the door, she moved everything to block the door and to keep them out.

Sam and Percy went down to Erin's room. They tried to open the door, but with no success.

Percy said, "Come on, we'll try later."

On the second day of not eating, the doctor, who went around to evaluate the patients in the institution, noticed that a tray of food was sitting outside of Erin's room door that had not been touched again.

He said to Erin, as he looked through the glass on the door, "You better eat or you're going starve to death if you don't."

Erin never changed her expression. She continued to look in the opposite direction away from all of the workers who came to the room knocking on the door, with the exception of one young man who attended the same school that Erin was attending. He was a young black gay guy; whose name was Sean. He sometimes called himself Séance. He was one who loved to be seen. Sean would sometimes go overboard with his behavior when others were around. He would sashay around and move like a ballerina.

Erin talked to him because they got along well in school and he promised her that he would keep what they talked about among themselves.

On graduation day, they started talking, and then Erin expressed how she felt about this day not having Destiny, along with her other sisters, walking across the stage.

Sean told Erin how he felt about all that had happened to her and her sisters. He did not think that it was right for the state to accuse her for the disappearance of the four guys who attacked her and her sisters.

Sean expressed how he hated bullies. He said, "You know I have been bullied for a long time. I don't bother anyone. I have the same body parts like everyone else. I laugh. I cry. I dream. The only difference is I'm attracted to the same sex. Love has no gender. You love who you want to love. I pray and only God knows the answer, and He is the only one that will judge me in the end. I go to church. I pay my tithes, and the church doesn't give it back to me!"

Another thing Sean said that really had Erin's full attention was when he said, "I will never understand how the law can come to your home, lock you up, and do nothing to the four boys who killed your sister. You know race plays a big ugly part in all of this and they know it. They just swept it under the rug and the law walked right on top of that same rug. Those four boys were told to stay away from you and your sisters, but what did they do? (Sean gave two snaps of the fingers as he walked swiftly in a circle.) They came around anyway!"

Then Sean said, "Back to you, baby girl. They are talking about how you have not eaten. Are you ok, honey? Do I need to call your parents or that fine brother of yours? You know I will go right over to your house and knock on the door. Yes, I will do just that."

"No, I'm ok, Sean. I'm on a mission. My family may not come by today, but I will see them tomorrow, and I'll be going home!" Erin said.

"Oh, you are? They are going to let you go?" Sean asked.

"They probably don't want to, but my dad, he doesn't play," Erin said.

Sean looked down the hall. He saw Sam, Percy, and Nancy coming. He told Erin that they were coming. Erin told Sean, "If they ask you if you heard me talk, tell them no. I have nothing to say to any of them. They tried to give me a shot for whatever. I had to clock them, that white lady and that fat black man."

"Ok, sweetie, you know I won't say a word," Sean replied.

"When you say clock them, what do you mean?" Sean asked.

"In this case, kick butt, get them straight," Erin said.

Sean covered his mouth, as he laughed and said, "No you didn't kick the white one's butt and the black one's butt. I wish I could have seen that!"

"Sean, why aren't you working, and why are you standing here talking to the Jackson girl? Did she say anything to you?" Percy asked.

"Percy, I do more work around here than any of the staff. Well, Percy, I have not gotten a word out of Erin's mouth yet. She was one of my classmates and I was talking about the fun times we had, trying to get her to say something," Sean answered.

"Miss Jackson, open this door. We need to come inside," Percy said.

Erin paid him no attention. She kept looking at Sean as he laughed and made faces while standing behind them.

"Ok, Sam. Help me push this door," Percy said.

So they pushed and pushed on the door a few times, but they had no luck.

"Come on, Sam. You are not helping me. I'm doing all this by myself," Percy said.

"Look, Percy, your body is barely touching the door and I am not about to keep pushing on this door and it's not budging. You look like you're going to pass out and you did nothing at all," Sam said.

"Come on, let's go. Yeah, I am a little tired. Oh well, we tried. If she talks and tells her story, fine. If she don't, what can we do?" Percy said, as they walked away.

"Percy, I think you're just a little lazy," Sam said.

"No, I'm a little smarter. That's why I'm the boss," Percy said.

"I really don't think you're the boss for that reason," Sam said.

Back at the Jackson's home, today was a happy, but sad day. It's the day that all the sisters looked forward to, graduation day. When the family got up, they all had mixed feelings. They had Destiny and Erin on their minds.

But then Aaron said, "This is the day that the Lord has made. We are going to rejoice, knowing that Destiny is with our Heavenly Father, and that it was not meant for her to walk across the stage today. But she is strutting on the streets paved with gold, wearing her heavenly robe and crown. I want you two to strut your stuff and know that your sister is looking down on you smiling. Think about how some of your dreams are now being fulfilled. Erin will get her diploma, but she just won't walk across the stage. Do you think that she is worried about walking across the stage? No, because she is on a mission. So I want you, Christian and you, Ebony to enjoy your day. Focus on good things."

"Very well said, son. This too shall pass. Girls, one of your sisters is gone and we will never forget her and your other sister. We're going to let her mission buy me that Cadillac and take all of us on a cruise. I want you girls to cheer up. Now, come give Grandma a big hug," Leslie said.

With lots of the family in the home, they all were feeling the same emptiness, but that didn't stop them from doing what they could to take the girls' minds off their sisters; and it seemed to cheer up both of them.

The family took pictures, before and after they ate breakfast, and then they headed to the university for the graduation.

Back at the mental institution, the shift leader, Percy, was an overweight white man, who was not very fond of people of color. His attitude towards some of the workers and patients, clearly says, "I don't like you." Percy was that kind of worker that came to work daily, always tired, and left work well-rested. He would sleep on the job and every time he opened his eyes after a nap, his mouth would open as well. He was always snacking on something, his entire shift.

Sean went down to the office to inform Percy that Erin had not eaten since she's been at the institution.

"Percy, are you aware that Miss Jackson hasn't eaten since she has been here?" he said.

Percy said, "Yes, I am. She was looking well to me. You can't make someone eat if they don't want to!"

"Erin has that door blocked for a reason. Why is she blocking her door, Percy?" Sean asked.

"Why aren't you working, Sean?" Percy said.

"If you look at the clock, I am off the clock, Percy. Have you called her parents to let them know that she's not eating, Percy?"

"If you are off the clock, then why are you still here, Sean? And the answer to your question is, no, I have not called her parents. Why am I telling you anyway?" Percy said.

"Maybe, because I asked you a question. That's what most people do. Answer a question," Sean said.

"You know, if I owned this business, half of you would not be working here," Percy said.

"Why Percy, why? Go right on ahead and say it, I dare you," Sean said.

Then Percy looked to the left and he looked to the right, and then he said, "No one is around. It's your word against mine. Because I don't like blacks or gays, that's why, period."

"Well Percy, I am only here because my degree is dealing with the mental mind and I see that one day, you will probably be one of my patients. But let me say this to you, Percy. It was your word against my recorder (then Sean pulled the recorder out of his pocket). You see, Percy, Erin and her sisters are friends of mine. They are beautiful black women, and you said that you have not called Erin's parents to tell them that their child has not eaten in two days and that she has herself barricaded in her bedroom. But before I go Percy, let me say this, Erin's parents do not play. They are going to come up here and take their child right out of here, but not before they tell you a thing or two. And Percy, don't hate blacks. We are strong and beautiful people. Just read our history, you would be amazed at what we have done for every race in the United States. Percy, you can't touch us!" Sean said.

"Sean, I think you better leave," Percy said.

Sean turned around and walked away with a smile on his face, saying to himself, "I got your fat white ass. Now Percy, let me see what you do when I stop by the Jackson's home before I come to work tomorrow, or should I go today? No, let the family enjoy their children's graduation day."

So the next day when Sean got up, it was early in the morning. He was due to be at work at 7:00 a.m., so he left his home by 6:30 a.m.

Sean said to himself, "I can't go by the Jackson's home this early and wake the whole house up. What I am going to do is go by their house on my lunchbreak. I'll show his fat ass. I am not playing with Percy."

When Sean arrived at work, his first stop was to see Erin. He looked in her room through the glass on the door. She was sleeping, so he did not want to disturb her, so he went on about his day. When lunchtime came for Sean, he went back to her room and said to her, "How are you feeling, Erin?"

"I'm ok, I've been drinking water from the sink," Erin said.

"Well honey, you can't chew water and it's sure not going to make you hockey or poo poo. That's what my grandma would say when we had to use the bathroom. All I'm saying is that you need some nutrients in your body, girl. I'll be back," Sean said.

Sean left the building and headed over to the Jackson's home. He went up to the door and rang the bell.

Ebony answered the door and said, "Hey, Sean!"

Sean said, "Congratulations, Ebony, how was the graduation?"

"It was good, long, and kind of emotional," she said.

"I can only imagine, but you made it through, and that's a good step," Sean said.

"What can I do for you, Sean?" she said.

"Well, Ebony, are your parents home?" Sean asked.

"Yes, they both are. Come on in, Sean," Ebony said.

Ebony walked Sean to the family room. Then she turned to look at

Sean and said, "Is everything ok?"

"I believe so, I just need to talk with your parents for a few minutes, while I'm on my lunchbreak," Sean answered.

"Have a seat, let me run upstairs and get them. They will be right down," Ebony said.

Aaron and Anita came down the stairs. Aaron said, "Hey, Sean, it's been a while since I last saw you!"

"It has. Hi, Mr. Jackson," Sean said.

"How are you, Sean?" Anita said.

"I am well, working, and this is my last year in school," Sean answered.

"Well congratulations to you. What brings you by today?" Anita asked.

"Well, Mr. and Mrs. Jackson, I work at the mental institution where Erin is. I didn't know that she was there until yesterday when I heard the workers talking about a patient who was not eating; so I wanted to see this person. When I went to see her, Erin told me that an orderly and a nurse came into her room trying to give her a shot, something that will make her talk. But like Erin said to me, she had to clock them. The nurse dropped the needle and Erin has it. Now she has barricaded herself in the room because she doesn't trust those people. I don't blame her for that because some of them are prejudiced individuals. She said that she has been drinking water, but I don't want her to get sick. I went to Percy, who is one of the team's leads, about Erin not eating and asked him if he'd called you. He said he could care less if Erin eats or not. And I want you to know that I have it on tape," Sean explained.

"I want to thank you, Sean, for stopping by to tell us what's going on. You said his name is Percy? We are heading to the institution as soon as we grab our things. Oh, you said this is your lunchbreak? Did you eat?" Mr. Jackson asked.

"No sir, I did not have the chance!" Sean answered.

"Christian is in the kitchen. There's some salad, chicken, and other food in there. Help yourself, grab a plate to go, and thanks again," Mr. Jackson said.

"Chris," Aaron yelled.

"Yes, Dad," Chris answered.

"Sean is coming in the kitchen. Fix him a plate to go and your mom and I are going to get Erin. We'll be back in a couple of hours. You can let the others know," Aaron said.

So Aaron and Anita left the house and headed to the mental institution.

Aaron said, "Before we go over to the institution, let me call Judge Kendra first. We may have to stop by her office for release papers."

So Aaron called Kendra and said, "Good afternoon, Judge Harrison, how are you?"

"Well, good afternoon to you, Attorney Jackson. I'm doing well, thanks for asking. How's the family holding up with all that has gone on?" Judge Harrison asked.

"We are holding it together, with the help from God above. Listen, you know my daughter was taken to the county jail for questioning about the disappearance of the four guys. Then she was taken to the mental institution because she did not talk to anyone. I have to make this short; and when we both have the time, I can go over everything with you. But let me say this, the arrest papers were incorrect. The four detectives that questioned Erin, well, Erin broke one of their wrists for touching her butt. She's now at the mental institution and she hasn't eaten. This is the third day. Nita gave them instructions to not medicate her and they tried anyway. Wow, let me get to the point. Will I need release papers to get my child out of that place?" Aaron asked.

"My, you were on a roll. I can tell that there's a lot on your plate. We really need to get together, sit down, and talk. Now the answer to your question is yes, but this seems like a big mess. Let's do this, why don't you head on to the institution and let them know that you are signing your child out? Now they are not supposed to give her to you without court papers, but I don't think that there are any papers. If they allow you to take her out without documentation, the whole system will be in hot water. Needless to say, they can be sued. Go try it, see what happens, and call me later," Kendra said.

When the Jacksons arrived at the mental institution, Jason was sitting at the desk. They walked over to him and said, "Hi, I am Aaron Jackson. I'm here to see and sign out my daughter, Erin Jackson."

"If you would go over to that door, I will buzz you in. Stop and see the person at the desk," Jason instructed.

Aaron and Anita walked over to the door and stood waiting for the buzzer. When it sounded, Aaron pulled the door open. Anita walked in and Aaron went behind her and they walked over to the desk, only to see Percy sleeping. It angered Aaron so much to the point of taking a picture. Aaron pulled out his phone and Anita tried to stop him, but he gave her an evil look. Even though she did not want him to take the picture, he did it anyway.

After he took the picture, he cleared his throat very loudly, trying to wake Percy. Percy did not move. The second time, he made a sneezing sound and Percy jumped and said, "Good afternoon, sorry I had my eyes closed; that's when I do my best thinking."

Aaron looked at the name plate on the desk with Percy's name on it and said, "Well Percy, you were thinking real hard. My wife and I have been standing here for a few minutes. We are Erin Jackson's parents, and we are here to discharge her. What room is she in?"

Percy pulled the book out, flipped through the pages, and said, "She's in room 122. That's straight down the hall to the right!"

Anita and Aaron headed down the hall. When they turned the corner, they heard Percy say, "Oh, Mr. and Mrs. Jackson, hold up. I'm coming with you."

"He said he's coming with us," Anita said.

"I heard him. He will catch up with us, because we are not stopping," Aaron answered. So they kept walking.

When her parents reached her room, Erin was standing over by the dresser where she hid the needle. The dresser had a mirror on it and she saw her parents looking through the glass.

She quickly grabbed the needle and put it down in her sock. She turned with a big smile on her face and she ran and started moving the furniture that was blocking the door.

"Look at my baby girl, putting herself through all this. I know that furniture is heavy and I know she's starving. I'm hurt right now. I really hate that I let her talk me into this," Aaron expressed to Anita.

As Anita rubbed Aaron on his back, she said, "I know it hurts you right now. It hurts me too, and all this will be behind us very soon."

Percy reached the room and said, "Oh, so now she moves the damn furniture!"

"Excuse me, Percy, what did you mean by that?" Aaron asked.

"Well, one of my workers and I tried to get in the room yesterday and we couldn't," he answered.

"Why has my daughter barricaded herself in this room?" Aaron asked.

"Well sir, it's beyond me," Percy said.

"Why didn't someone call me to let me know that you couldn't get into the room?" Aaron asked.

Erin opened the door. Anita hugged her and kissed her on the forehead. Anita asked, "Are you ok?"

"Yes, Mommy. I'm ok," Erin answered.

"Well, the workers couldn't get in to clean it, so we tried to get in and couldn't," Percy said.

"Percy, you can get in now and do all the cleaning you want, after I sign any papers to discharge my child from this place," Aaron said.

"We can go back down to the office," Percy said.

Aaron gave Erin a hug and asked, "Hi, baby, how are you?"

"I'm alright, Daddy," Erin answered.

"So now she talks," Percy said, as they walked down the hall.

"Oh, you haven't heard anything yet, Percy!" Aaron said.

When they got to the front desk, Percy went behind the counter and said, "There's really nothing to sign. I just need to go into the computer under her name and type discharged."

"Discharged, is that all? Nothing for my daughter or me to sign?" Aaron asked.

"Nothing for you to sign, sir, that's it," Percy said.

"Let's get out of here," Aaron said.

When Erin and her parents got into the car, Aaron said, "Baby girl, I hope that you never have another idea like this again. The state is going to hear from me very soon. This will be a case that's going to require a lot of my time and focus. I'm not letting them or those boys' parents get away with this. We are getting ready to be paid dearly!"

"Erin, that reminds me, give me that needle," Anita asked.

Erin handed her the needle and said, "Dad, did I tell you we are going to be rich?"

Aaron said, "You know, I hate all this has happened. My child is gone. She didn't even have a chance to start her career. Something that should not have even started, dealing with four lame brain boys. People like that you can only pray for them. Their parents were probably afraid of them, and now I have to plan for a funeral. These people don't know, but the fight is just beginning!"

Within four days, the Jacksons prepared and had a memorial service for Destiny. It was held at the funeral home. Many people loved and cared for Destiny. Friends, co-workers, and neighbors of the family all attended. They cried, sang, and laughed as they told stories about Destiny.

The next day, after the service, Destiny's body was flown to South Carolina where the family held the funeral service at Mount Anna Baptist Church. And there, she was laid to rest in her family's hometown.

On that same day, Aaron got on the phone and called his office. Angie, his receptionist, answered, "Law office, this is Angie speaking, how may I help you?"

"Angie, hi, this is Aaron!"

"Oh, hi, Mr. Jackson. The service for Destiny was really nice. How's the family doing?"

"We are all ok, considering what happened. It's been two months and my child is finally going to be laid to rest. Look Angie, I know that Phillip had to go to the Aiken office and Cindy is out on maternity leave. I'm going to need Mason, Kennan, and Stan to do some work for me every chance they get. I'm going to drop off all the information for the cases that are being built up. I'll make copies of them and leave them on my desk. Now, I need them to look into the background of the four boys who attacked my girls. I don't need to say all that's needed to build up a case. I'm going to need information on the mental institution, the county jail, any wrongdoings, and any complaints or lawsuits. I need everything you all can find on Detectives Arthur Fisher, Myron Greyson, Alexander McNeill, and Early Eborn. They are the ones who questioned Erin," Aaron said.

"I will give them this message. You don't have to worry. We will take care of this while you are away," Angie said.

"Thanks, Angie. I'll see you later today," Aaron said, as their call ended.

Meanwhile, at the Jackson's house, Anita was getting ready to go take the syringe to the hospital's lab to find out what the mental institution was going to inject Erin with. Anita planned to see Taylor, the technician.

When Anita arrived at the hospital, she went straight to the lab where Taylor was testing multiple samples. She put on the sterile gear from head to toe and went inside the lab.

"Hey, Taylor, I know that you are busy, but I need a big favor. This syringe is filled with something. Can you please test it for me and let me know what's in it?" Anita said.

"Where did it come from?" Taylor asked.

"This is what the mental institution tried to give Erin, but she kicked it out of their hands," Anita answered.

"Let's get right on that now!" Taylor replied.

"Oh, you can do it right now? I will need a copy of what it is and how it's used!" Anita said.

"Oh sure, no problem," Taylor answered.

It took about 30 minutes for the lab results to come.

Taylor said, "The results are printing now. Wow, I don't believe this. In this syringe, there were two types of medication – both for depression and anxiety. It is used to control how the brain thinks and to slow the brain function down. What they probably were going to do was use hypnosis on Erin. The two drugs are Sertraline (generic Zoloft) and Nortriptyline (generic Pamelor). Now this one (she pointed to the Nortriptyline) is stronger and the side effects can be blurred vision, constipation, and drowsiness. It can also lower your blood pressure, and if they give too much, it could be fatal!"

With tears in Nita's eyes, she said, "Oh God, I can't lose another child!"

"Well, it's a good thing that Erin did kick the needle out of their hands. Cheer up, she's ok!" Taylor said.

"I know, I was just thinking how thankful I am that she responded the way she did. Those people at that mental institution are in for a rude awakening. I've got to run. I need to call Aaron and tell him. Then I got to get myself ready to head out of town," Anita said.

"When are you coming back? When is vacation over?" Taylor asked.

"Believe me, none of it was a vacation. It seemed like everything was happening back to back. But after all this is over, we are going to take a real vacation," Anita said.

"You and your family deserve one. I know you have been through a lot. Go on, enjoy the rest of the day, and I'll see you tomorrow," Taylor said.

Anita gave Taylor a hug and she said, "Thanks for everything."

Anita called Aaron. He answered the phone, "Hey, babe. Is everything ok?"

"Yes, I'm leaving the lab, heading home with the results in that syringe!" Anita said.

"Awesome, can you tell me when I get home? I'm finishing up some papers before we head out of town," Aaron said.

"Sure, I'll see you when you get home. I love you," Anita said.

"I love you too, babe. Bye," Aaron said.

"Bye, bye," Anita said.

Back at the mental institution, Percy, Nancy, and Sam were being reprimanded for not being able to retrieve the needle that was left in Erin's room.

Ennis, the head of the mental institution, was walking on pens and hot rocks because he was wondering what problems down the road he could be facing due to this negligence.

The family members that came for the graduation also stayed for Destiny's service. They were headed home to prepare themselves for her funeral service in South Carolina.

Four and One

GOING THROUGH, WHEN IT'S ALL SAID AND DONE

Chapter Seven

Aaron Jr. was keeping busy, job hunting, and trying to figure out how things happened the way that they did. He was not happy with the way things were handled during the time his sisters were being bullied. He didn't like the way the police officers conducted themselves during Destiny's investigation or the way Erin's arrest was handled. He was not a fan of how the media and the bystanders performed during Erin's time at the police station.

When Aaron Jr. joined the Air Force, he moved up rank really quickly. The Air Force allowed him to enroll into acceleration classes. He wanted to be all that he could be in a short period of time.

He studied Law Enforcement and Forensic Science, because he wanted to know how the laws of each state were written and how evidence is collected, tested, presented, and stored.

He wanted to learn everything that would make him the best at what he wanted to become for his future.

While in the military, Aaron Jr. met Lisa. She too, was in the Air Force. They were a nice pair and worked well together.

Lisa and Aaron were engaged to be married, but they didn't set a date for the wedding yet.

Lisa's job was in Cyber Security and Biochemistry, where she maintained the computer functions a few days a week, and the other half of the week, she worked in the lab testing all human body samples.

When the family arrived in South Carolina for Destiny's funeral service, it was a sad but happy occasion. The Jacksons were glad to be back home, spending time with childhood friends, neighbors, and just feeling love from everyone.

During the hours of viewing, before the service began, Aaron and Anita became overjoyed when they saw some of the teachers that taught their children. They traveled from D.C. to come and express their love and sympathy to the family. There was Mr. Demps, the gym teacher, who also coached gymnastics and track and field, Sensei Raymond, the martial artist, Mr. Brown, Ms. Beasley, Mr. Hendricks, and Ms. Lamor'e. The children learned all of the different languages that they spoke from Ms. Lamor'e. All of those teachers played important roles in the Jackson's children's lives. Those teachers cared about the children's future.

Police officers, in uniform – Jeff, Brian, Marques, and Tyree surprised Aaron and Anita. They had no idea that they got the ok from the funeral home to be the pallbearers.

Judge Freda and her husband Samuel were at the funeral. Dr. Franklin, Taylor, Trisha, and so many others traveled to attend Destiny's funeral.

The funeral service was beautiful. The eulogy was given by Pastor Penny. Destiny loved to dance, so the church's praise dancers danced to one of the songs that Destiny loved, "We Shall Behold Him." Mrs. Blackmon's solo was, "I'm Happy With Jesus Alone." Corky, one of Anita's friends, sang, "The Battle Is the Lord's."

When the service came to a close, the choir started to sing, "I'll Fly Away," and the funeral home directors signaled for Jeff, Tyree,

Marques, and Brian to come forward. Those men were in coordination, and when I say coordination, I mean they got their step in. What an amazing sight to see.

After the burial, which was on the church grounds, they all came together for the repast that was held. Inside and outside of the church, everyone talked, laughed, and exchanged numbers.

Aaron walked over to the speaker and said, "May I have everyone's attention? Nita and I want to express our sincere thanks to each one of you. We realize that you don't have to see a person or even talk with them daily to know that they love you. My daughter Destiny went home to be with our Heavenly Father over two months ago. So many of you loved and cared about Destiny; you've traveled a long distance to be with us today. That lets me know that you love us, and we love you too. May God keep right on blessing each one of you. Thank you."

Everyone walked around and mingled. Aaron walked behind Jeff and grabbed him.

"Brother, y'all never cease to amaze me. That was a beautiful thing y'all did. Thanks man, I'll never forget it!" Aaron said.

"Ah, man, you know how we roll. That's what brothers are for. No need to say thanks. We are family," Jeff said.

After Aaron and his family spent a few days in South Carolina, they returned home to Florida.

The following week, Anita went back to work, but Aaron went back right away. He worked at home and in the office. He did not take on any new cases while he focused on his mission. He was determined to address all the wrong that his family endured.

Once all the research and the investigations were completed, Aaron went over to meet with Judge Freda. They ate lunch together.

Judge Freda read over all of the documents and said to Aaron, "You are very sharp. Like they say, you got them by the balls. I know these cases are winners. You know that I can't respond to any of this, but I do want to say, 'You go boy.' Get them for all that you can. I am so happy for you and your family. You all have been through a lot, and when you win, congrats to each one of you."

After Aaron's meeting with the judge ended, he headed down to the courthouse and filed papers against the state, the mental institution, Ennis (who heads the institution), Nancy, Percy, Sam, the police department, the detectives (Arthur Fisher, Myron Greyson, Alexander McNeill, and Early Eborn), and the parents of Peter Pitts, Richard Rivers, Billy Goldstein, and Bobby Spinks, on behalf of Erin, Christian, Destiny, and Ebony Jackson.

The charges ranged from false arrest, assault with the intent to do bodily harm in the first degree, attempted murder, murder in the first degree, damage of property, mental anguish, bullying, obstruction, failure to follow stay away orders, improper handling of a suspect, and the list went on. Aaron filed a separate suit against Detective Myron Greyson for sexual harassment.

It was close to a year and the Jacksons were still in court. Aaron knew that it would take some time. He had many cases filed against a lot of people and businesses.

The first case that was heard was against the police department. They were hit with so many wrongdoings that the chief deputy of the police department resigned from his position.

The chief's deputy assistant, who took orders from the chief and passed them down to the departments for the state of Florida, resigned because of mistreatment of blacks, not only civilians, but uniformed officers, as well.

Weeks later, after all of the negative reports about the state's police department, the commissioner resigned, so then all three positions were temporarily ran by the other high-ranking officers.

It was announced on every news station that the state of Florida was looking to fill the vacant seat for a commissioner to head the police department and the positions that were currently temporarily held. A permanent replacement would be appointed by the new commissioner, and then a website address and phone number flashed across the screen. Aaron Jr. wrote the information down and applied for the position.

With all the training and his educational background, Aaron Jr. became the first black man to head the police departments in the state of Florida.

This was a very big responsibility for him, because every state, city, and town had its own laws. With a black man as the head, leading and commanding this position, it did not go well with many white officers that had been in the department for many years.

Many officers retired. Some changed professions, while others stayed and tried to get along with the other new black recruits that were trained and started working soon after so many left the department.

Lisa moved to Florida, just in time for Aaron Jr. to be sworn in. She was working for the NASA Air and Space Center and living in another town with her brother and his family, which was about an hour and a half away from where Aaron Jr. lived.

She was happy that she and Aaron Jr. reunited because they both were looking forward to their promising future together.

On Monday, Aaron Jr. was sworn in. The celebration went better than the negative thinkers thought. Even though Junior was currently left holding an empty basket, with no leaders under him, he did not fret. He knew that God was going to place it on his heart and put the right leaders in his path.

When Aaron Jr. moved into his new office, he hung paintings and pictures. He also added books in the bookcase.

Reading and researching African American History was one subject that he loved.

In the back of Commissioner Jackson's head, he remembered how his family and other people were treated when he was a child and all the way through adulthood. So he told himself, "This madness has to stop!" He was tired of the way black people were being treated.

Aaron Jr. reflected back on stories told to him about how blacks were never recognized for the accomplishments that they made, inventions that they made, and how so many lost their life's treasures because of lack of knowledge. In his heart, he wanted to make a positive change in the justice system.

With the deep passionate love for righteousness, it felt like a thorn in Aaron Jr.'s side, especially when he would read or hear that women had been raped, children were being kidnapped or abused, and females who were forced to sell their bodies on the streets. He hated the fact that drugs were being smuggled into this country and that people were too weak to say no. Firearms were getting into the wrong hands, people were stealing other people's property, and many police departments had dirty cops on their force. All these things and more, made him pray even more. He vowed to make a change. He made a vow to God and himself. He believed that as long as he was covered by the blood of Jesus and angels encamped around him, God would continue to order his steps. He knew he would make a change in the state where he lived.

On Wednesday, Junior and Lisa met after they both ended work early. They discussed wedding plans while they drove around looking at the different home developments that were being built. They stopped and looked inside of a few model homes. There was one home in a gated community that they both loved, so they talked with the agent, went over the floor plan, looked at all the amenities that the developer offered, and they added up the cost for any upgrades.

Aaron Jr. and Lisa walked around the house a second time, looking inside and outside. They wanted to make sure that they both agreed on everything.

"I love the area," Aaron Jr. said. "It's quiet in this gated community. They have security, so any guest would have to stop at the gate while security contacts the homeowner before being allowed to enter. We have whatever we need in driving distance. What do you think, Lisa?"

"I love it. I think we should go for it," she said.

So after they walked around a third time discussing changes that they would love to make in their home, they both went back inside and sat down with the realtor. All of the changes in their new home were made at that time – the carpet for each room, the cabinets for the kitchen, the style for each bathroom, the tile for the floors, and the marble flooring for the foyer were chosen. Aaron Jr. and Lisa decided on the phone, TV, and alarm locations.

After all that was done, a handshake closed the deal. They both walked out with all the needed information on the changes made, copies of the contract, along with business cards and a number to call if they wanted to make any changes within thirty days.

At the end of the day, Lisa drove back to her brother's house, and

Aaron Jr. went home. He was still living with his family.

On Thursday, while Aaron Jr. and his family were home sitting at the table having dinner, Anita said, "We are all so proud of you. Let's invite some of our friends over on Saturday for a celebration cookout. What do you all think?"

Aaron said, "I think that's a good idea."

Aaron Jr. said, "I think that's a wonderful idea, now I won't have to call a meeting. I can make some of my announcements on Saturday!"

Ebony said, "That would be great. I have to work this Saturday and my boss is asking when I am going to do a live broadcasting. If it's ok, can I do it here?"

"Sure. What do you think, Mom and Dad?" Junior asked.

Aaron hunched his shoulders and said, "Fine with me. What about you, Nita?"

"I think it will be a good experience for you, Ebony," Anita said.

"Is this going to be heard over the radio?" Erin asked.

"Yes, and we are going to have cameras so that it's seen on the television as well. That's why I'm so excited!" Ebony said.

"So, can we advertise what we do, our professions, to gain more business?" Christian asked.

"Yes, that is the reason I want to do this. We are going to have lots of fun. Now we have to call and invite people!" Ebony said.

"I can make my announcements. Ooooh boy, wait until y'all hear what I have to say!" Junior said.

They all said at the same time, "We can't wait!"

So Friday after breakfast, they all started calling people they wanted to invite. Junior overheard his dad talking with Jeff, so he interrupted and said, "Dad, will you tell Uncle Jeff to let Tyree, Marques, and Brian know. Oh, and tell them to come early."

"Ok, you heard what Junior said, right?" Aaron asked Jeff.

"I heard every word," Jeff answered.

"Good, that way I don't have to repeat what he said," Aaron replied.

Erin, Ebony, and Christian invited their friends and co-workers. Anita invited her personal friends and some of her work friends. Aaron invited Thurman, Judge Freda and her husband, his employees, and some other friends.

After Aaron finished talking on the phone, his cell phone rang and it was Luke, one of the attorneys at the law firm.

Aaron answered, "Hey, Luke. How did it go?"

"Great! The four detectives, we got them running scared. All of these lawsuits. We had three courtrooms tied up today. I just saw Kennan. He's going to call you. What he told me is that the state saw all of their wrongdoings on paper. I haven't talked with Cindy. I believe she's still in court. I just wanted to call and update you on what's going on down here," Luke said.

"I had no doubt. I knew all of it would be done in order. I hope you can stop by on Saturday. We're having a little get together in honor of Junior's new job. Would you do me a favor and let the others know? I'm making calls now, but I don't want to leave anyone out. Everything's kicking off around 1:00. Thanks, Luke. We will all talk on tomorrow," Aaron said.

On that Saturday morning, the whole family woke up early and got things together in the yard and around the house. They prepared the food and set up the chairs and tables. They had the music playing. They were really excited about this celebration. It was something that was well-needed after all that they had gone through.

Ebony left the house for work, but she was due to come back around 11:30 to have lunch. She and her co-workers, before they could eat, had to set up the cameras and equipment that would be used for the broadcast.

When Ebony arrived home with her co-workers, she introduced all four of them to the family. Ebony showed them where the equipment could be set up and they went right to work.

Jeff, Tyree, Brian, and Marques were the first to show up. Aaron walked up to each man, gave them some dap, and said, "Thanks, I knew you guys would be here before anyone else!"

"You knew we had to come and see if we could help in any way. That's what brothers do for each other. We will never leave family hanging!" Tyree said.

"Now, what can we do to help?" Brian asked.

"Well first, Marques, I know what you love doing; so fire up the grill. The meats are in the refrigerator. We have some drinks in the coolers, but we're going to need that dry ice chopped up. Look, y'all have entertained before, whatever you see that needs to be done, go for it. Oh, Junior has some big announcements to make, so he wanted to make sure that all four of you were here!" Aaron said.

The family, friends, and guests started to arrive. Everyone was excited. The grill was smoking and the music was playing. Some were dancing, while others were sitting or walking around mingling with each other.

The cameraman was recording the function and then Ebony came and told everyone, with the mic in her hand, "Good afternoon everybody, I'm going to introduce myself only, because my sisters and I look so much alike. I am Ebony, and I want to thank you all for attending today's celebration in honor of my dear brother, Aaron Jr. I'm sure we all know by now that my brother was chosen to be the commissioner for the state of Florida and we are celebrating today in his honor. Commissioner Jackson, will you stand?"

Commissioner Jackson stood and waved his hand, as Ebony made her way to him. She put the mic to her mouth and said, "Would you like to say something?"

"First, I want to thank my Lord and Savior for making all this possible. I thank Him for bringing my family through the storm. I thank Him for being our Anchor. I want to say that I am happy for my new job. I want to be fair with all of my employees. I know that racism still lives, even today, but I will not tolerate it in any department in the state of Florida. I want each officer to know that he or she can come to any one of my leading heads in confidence to tell about any wrongdoings. We will look into it and handle it accordingly.

"Currently, there are four positions that need to be filled. I have names of four men who have shown dignity, courage, pride, and they have shown me what a real officer is. At this time, I want to introduce to everyone who is listening or watching this live announcement, my Chief Deputy will be former police officer, Jeffery Harrison; my Assistant Chief Deputy will be former police officer, Tyree Brown; my Captain, will be former police officer Marques Bellamy; and my Lieutenant will be former police officer, Brian Thompson. Gentlemen, will you all stand?" Commissioner Jackson said.

Marques, Jeff, Brian, and Tyree had no idea of any of this, so they were still in shock, as they and their wives shared tears of joy. Ebony and Junior walked over to where all four of them were sitting and said,

"Can we congratulate these four men by giving them a hand clap?"

"On Tuesday morning, I will need to see each one of you in my office for the swearing-in ceremony. My leaders will be wearing their dress uniform. I have copies of the program. You may invite guests. Congratulations to each one of you for going above and beyond the call of duty. Would you like to comment?"

Jeff stood and said, "I am truly overwhelmed and humbled. Never in my wildest dreams would I have even thought that this day would come true. But, I believe if I let my light so shine, people would see my good works, and God answers my prayers. I thank you."

Tyree stood and said, "I don't think my speech will be as good as Officer Harrison's. Excuse me, should I say Chief Deputy Harrison's, speech? But, I am happy today, this was really unexpected. I accept the position with joy. God never fails. He saw my need, He answered my prayers, and all I can say is, 'Thank you, Lord.'"

Marques stood next and said, "What can I say? Most people know how I love cooking on the grill, so I thought I was invited here today to do just that. But this news today lets me know that every day when I leave my home, none of us know if we will return home. But when I get out on the streets, I give an encouraging word to everyone I meet. One of my favorite verses in this song that I love is, *Lift Him Up.*" Marques held his hands together and said, "God, I thank you for bringing this young man in my life. I thank you."

"And last but not least," Commissioner Jackson said, as he handed the mic to Brian. Brian began singing, "'*Thank You, Lord.*' I am truly grateful to you Commissioner Jackson because you are a Godsend. I humbly accept the lieutenant's position with deep pride, and I will be the best man for the job that I can be. Thank you."

"Well, you heard it. Commissioner Jackson has just appointed his new

Chief Deputy, the Assistant Chief Deputy, his Captain, and his Lieutenant. Congratulations to each one of you. Recording live from the Jackson's family home, this is Ebony Jackson. We will return, but now we are going to hand it over to the studio."

The celebration went well and everyone enjoyed themselves. Junior announced to the family that he and Lisa were planning to get married but a date had not been set. He also let the family know that they were having a home built.

When the celebration was over and the guests started to leave, Jeff, Brian, Marques, and Tyree stayed behind to help the family clean up.

Aaron said to Jeff, "Didn't I tell you that blessings were coming to all four of you, in a mighty way. I didn't know how, but He showed it to all four of you today!"

"Man, this was the best Christmas gift, the best birthday gift, it's just the best gift. This promotion was nothing but a blessing," Tyree said.

"I second that," Jeff said.

"Well, Brian man, I guess we third and fourth that. What you think?" Marques asked.

"You know I'm on board," Brian answered.

Tuesday morning came and all four men were sworn in by the mayor and many others were on site for the ceremony.

The trial against the four boys who attacked the sisters had started. It lasted three weeks. Even though the courts had evidence showing that they committed the murder of Destiny, with the absence of the four guys, the attorneys who represented them argued their case, stating that without their clients being present, the case should be thrown out of court.

This case was being heard by Judge Freda Perkins and she was not standing for any nonsense.

The Judge said, "After the senseless attacks on the sisters and the damage that was done to their car, I ordered all four of the young men to stay away from the Jackson girls. And I held each one of their parents responsible if any of them came in contact with any of the Jackson girls. They not only went against my order, but they committed murder to an innocent young lady, who did not graduate because they wanted to go around bullying people. I have signed documents by each parent of all four of these young men and it reads, 'To the parents of Peter Pitts, Bobby Spinks, Billy Goldstein, and Richard Rivers, you are being held responsible for any actions, or any wrongdoings brought on to any of the Jackson girls: Ebony, Christian, Destiny, or Erin. Your sons are not allowed to be at the school where the Jackson sisters attend. Your sons are not allowed to come within one thousand feet where any of the Jackson girls are present. If for any reason, this order is broken, and there is hurt, danger, death, damage, mental stress, verbal abuse, or any physical harm is done to the Jackson sisters, you, the parents of the four named young men, will be charged.

"There is no price that can be put on a life lost, but the surviving family members will be able to go on knowing that any action that lead to death caused by any one of your sons, will be charged. In my courtroom, I get a lot of cases of people being bullied. I don't like it. I never have and I never will. If your sons didn't know any better, you should have taught them. If you didn't know any better, you should have learned before any of you even thought about having sex. You should have kept your underclothes pulled up and picked up a book.

"I hate to imagine all that these four young ladies' parents went through. I am sorry for the loss of your child. (She turned to look at the Jackson family, then she turned and looked at the parents of the four guys.) Now, what I am about to say to each one of you is that I will give you six months to satisfy this judgment. Mr. and Mrs. Rivers, I order you to pay $450,000 to Mr. and Mrs. Jackson. If it is not paid in the six months, the courts will seize your assets.

"Mr. and Mrs. Goldstein, I order you to pay Mr. and Mrs. Aaron Jackson $450,000.

"Mr. and Mrs. Spinks, I order you to pay Mr. and Mrs. Aaron Jackson $450,000.

"And Mr. and Mrs. Pitts, I order you to pay Mr. and Mrs. Jackson $450,000.

"Now, Mr. and Mrs. Jackson, you still have three daughters. They have graduated from college. This money will not bring your child back, please use the money in any way that you both see fit."

Then, the Honorable Judge Freda Perkins said, as she slammed down the mallet, "Judgment for the plaintiff, and so it is ordered, it is written." She got up from her chair and walked out of the court.

For many weeks, Aaron was tied up in court dealing with his own family's cases.

The case against the police department for false arrest, failure to present proper papers, stress, humiliation, failure to follow the proper protocol when arresting and holding a suspect, all this and more was fought and won. In the case of the state's police department, the Jacksons were awarded $6,000,000.

The case against Detectives Arthur Fisher, Myron Greyson, Alexander McNeill, and Earley Eborn went on for close to a month. They were charged with failure to report the misconduct of a fellow officer, falsifying papers, covering up improper behavior, failure to request for the proper monitoring protocol. All of these charges, along with other charges, were brought against these four detectives, and the court ordered each detective to pay $160,000.

Detective Myron Greyson was also charged with an additional charges of attempted sexual assault. He was ordered to pay Erin $1,275,000. He boohooed, I mean he cried, as he wiped the tears from his eyes with his jacked-up hand and wrist.

In the case against the mental institution and its workers that were involved, Percy, Nancy, Sam, and Ennis were all charged for improper treatment of a patient, failure to follow the doctor's orders by attempting to medicate a patient that could have been a deadly injection, starvation of a client, not following proper protocol by not contacting the person listed on the admittance form to inform them that their loved one had not eaten. This case lasted close to one month and a half.

When it was all said and done with the court cases that were filed, the Jacksons won every case. In all of their lawsuits, it totaled up to $219,000,000 in compensation.

EPILOGUE

With some of this money, the Jacksons started the Destiny Jackson Crisis Center, one in Florida and one in Washington, D.C. In this center, licensed and trained workers counsel individuals who are or have been bullied, harassed, or assaulted on how to cope with the name calling, how to defend themselves, who to call if needed, and what to say.

Sean is now the head of Behavior Health. He's also being taught martial arts and mind control by all of the Jackson children in their spare time.

Erin works with a team of doctors who specializes in Sports Medicine, which consists of therapy, counseling, surgery, and repairing minor injuries in professional athletics. This business has grown so much that they now help others who are not athletes but have similar injuries.

Erin went back to school to become a doctor in her field. She plans to open up her own practice.

Christian started using her share and more of the settlement monies. She sat down with her parents and told them her dream of owning her own funeral homes; but she wanted to put them in the states that had the most crimes. Both parents thought it was a good idea, but they wanted her to research the cost to do what she was asking. She was undecided, but she knew any money that would be put out would come back quickly. She went as far as looking for land to buy.

When she came back to her parents with all of her findings, they thought it was a great idea and so they went for it. Christian now owns land in three states, where construction will soon start removing trees and building all that will be needed for the cemeteries. She found a building that was once a funeral home close to Baltimore, Maryland, that she will reopen. Christian plans to have a funeral home built in Illinois and Florida.

Anita and Aaron are thinking about moving back to South Carolina, and leaving the home that is for family vacation. They feel that their reason for moving to Florida is now complete.

The construction for Junior and Lisa's home has started and has been paid in full by his parents. Aaron and Anita even gave them a check to furnish their home.

The state has become a better place to live in, now that all the bad officers are no longer on the force. Now you have police officers to show the citizens that they care and can be trusted.

Jobs are becoming available, career centers are in place, GED programs are set up, and activity programs for youth and adults are open with all types of sports and activities. Crime is now at its lowest.

Erin went back to South Carolina. Her main focus was to go to the cemetery and visit with her sister. She sat by her sister's tombstone. "Des, sorry, I didn't get the chance to come see you sooner. My heart is still heavy knowing that the chain is broken. I miss you so much," she said.

As Erin started to cry, she said, "You know I am so glad that Mom and Dad put us in all the classes that they did. It allowed us to become stronger. It has helped me to see that it was not all about me. I am so sorry that you fell when we ran from those guys. But, you know, and I believe, because you live in me, you are always with me and you felt my pain when those boys snatched you, raped you, and broke your neck. When they did all that to you, I want you to know that I gave each one of them the same thing back. I clocked every last one. When I say I did them in, I mean I did them in. Mama and Daddy could not stop me because they know how my level of anger was at that time. But sister, now I can say, I can rest knowing that what they did to you and got away with it, or so they thought, it made me even madder. I don't think the police even looked for them at all. If I found each one of them as easy as I did, I know the police could have arrested them. So, you know that did not digest well with me. I did what I felt had to be done. If I didn't stop them, they would have come for all of us again, and I didn't want us to go through what happened to you ever again. No one will have to worry about those troublesome bullies again."

Then Erin said, "I've enrolled back into school getting my doctorate's degree. Now I can go on with my dream. I will never stop thinking about you. You will forever live in my heart, Des. You made me stronger. You made me a better young lady, and I will love you forever and ever. It's getting dark so I got to go. I will come and talk with you soon. I think the next time will be on our birthday. I know Chris and Ebony will come along with me. Goodbye for now, I love you, Des."

FINAL NOTES

Based On A True Story

Back in the sixties, racism was bad and the blacks knew it. But they also knew if they minded their own business, maybe the racist folks would not bother them. Yet, still that did not stop the white man or woman from calling the grown adults and children out of their name.

Years ago, in the South, the Ku Klux Klan (KKK) kicked their way into my great-grandfather's house looking for my grandfather. We all know what kind of intentions the KKK have towards people of color. They wanted to kill my granddad. While my grandfather was in the other room, we were told that my great granddad dropped to his knees and started praying. My family said he prayed so hard, so loud, and so long, that when he said, "Amen," the KKK were gone. It's no secret what God can do.

No matter who you are or what you have done, God is still on the throne, and you can call on Him anytime. No man is greater than our Heavenly Father.

Even though the people in this book grew up poor, like so many blacks did, the faith they had made them rich. The prayers that they sent up, oh boy! You can't mess with or touch God's anointed children.

NOTES

Song Titles Mentioned

Pg. (41) "You Are So Beautiful" – Written by Billy Preston and Bruce Fisher. (1974)

Pg. (43) "Here Comes the Bride" – Written by Richard Wagner (1850)

Pg. (123) "If I Can Help Somebody" – Written by Alma Bazel Androzzo. (1945)

Pg. (164) "I Need Thee Every Hour" - Written by Annie Sherwood Hawks. (1872)

Pgs. (200, 233) "The Battle Is the Lord's" – Written by Yolanda Adams (1993)

Pg. (200) "Yield Not to Temptation" - Written by Horatio R. Palmer. (1868)

Pg. (200) "Life's Railway to Heaven" - Written by M.E. Abbey. (1891).

Pg. (233) "I'll Fly Away" – Written by Albert E. Brumley (1929)

Pg. (233) "I'm Happy With Jesus Alone" – Written by Charles Prince Jones (1906)

Pg. (233) "We Shall Behold Him" – Written by Dottie Rambo (1980)

Pg. (243) "Lift Him Up" – Written by Johnson Oatman, Jr. (1903)

Pg. (243) "Thank you, Lord" – Written by J. Jefferson Cleveland.

ABOUT THE AUTHOR

Theresa Ann Boddie, born the sixth child of eight siblings, was raised by both parents, Ernest and M. Helen Boddie, in Washington, D.C. She currently lives in Fort Washington, Maryland. She is the mother of one son, Von.

After working many years with Verizon Communication as a Services Technician, she retired.

Theresa loves to laugh and make others laugh, but she has struggled with shyness within herself, from childhood through adulthood, which hindered her from fulfilling many dreams. However, Theresa is still a big dreamer, and she's always on a mission, completing one project and starting another.

Theresa strives to be the best that she can be. She shows it in many ways; she tries to let her light so shine by doing missionary work, blessing others with a cheerful word, and by sharing and/or giving from her heart. Going to church and working in the church as an usher and nurse in Her Father's house, where God's Word dwells, gives her strength.

Connect with the Theresa Boddie
Email: theresaboddie@hotmail.com
Facebook: Theresa Boddie-Ceaser

Four and One

www.ingramcontent.com/pod-product-compliance
Lightning Source LLC
Chambersburg PA
CBHW011141290426
44108CB00022B/2707